Magnetic Communities

Prospering Locally in a Global Economy

Magnetic Communities

Prospering Locally in a Global Economy

Larry Moolenaar

Printed in the United States of America

Cover Design: BVS Designs

Editor: LPW Editing & Consulting Services, LLC
www.litapward.com

First Printing, 2019

ISBN-13: 978-0-578-43126-0

For Rande,

Her encouragement and input

Contents

List of Illustrations   ix

Preface   xiii

Introduction   1

Part 1: Economics of Prosperity   11
   Chapter 1: Money Flow   17
   Chapter 2: Money Trail   29
   Chapter 3: New Money   33
   Chapter 4: Multipliers   41

Part 2: Magnetic Community Strategies   47
   Chapter 5: Community Strategies   55
   Chapter 6: Business Strategies   67
   Chapter 7: Tourist Strategies   93
   Chapter 8: Resident Strategies   111
   Chapter 9: Retiree Strategies   127
   Chapter 10: Government Strategies   137

A Fish Story   147

Summary   153

About the Author   163

List of Illustrations

1. Nonresidents Purchase Goods and Services from Local Businesses — 6

2. Residents Purchase Goods and Services from Local Businesses — 7

3. Money Flow – Stable Local Economy — 19

4. Money Flow – Growing Local Economy — 21

5. Money Flow – Shrinking Local Economy — 23

6. The Value of Manufacturing Wages — 36

7. The Value of Local Government Wages — 37

8. Locally Owned Businesses Sell Goods and Services to Customers Outside the Local Economy — 72

9. Local Businesses, Not Locally Owned, Sell Goods and Services to Customers Outside the Local Economy — 73

10. Locally Owned Businesses Sell Goods and Services to Local Customers — 80

11. Local Businesses, Not Locally Owned, Sell Goods and Services to Local Customers — 81

12. Local Businesses Purchase Goods and Services from Local Suppliers — 82

13. Local Businesses Purchase Goods and Services from Suppliers Outside the Local Economy — 84

14. Local Businesses Employ Residents — 88

15. Local Businesses Employ Nonresidents — 89

16. Tourists Purchase Goods and Services from Local   98
    Businesses

17. Local Art Gallery Sells Painting by Resident Artist   106

18. Local Art Gallery Sells Painting by Nonresident   107
    Artist

19. Residents Commute to Jobs Outside the Local   113
    Economy

20. Residents are Paid from Sources Outside the   115
    Local Economy

21. Residents Receive and Spend Government   119
    Transfer Payments

22. Residents Purchase Goods and Services from   124
    Local Businesses

23. Residents Purchase Goods and Services from   125
    Businesses Outside the Local Economy

24. Retirees Receive Retirement Income   133

25. Local Governments Collect Taxes from Residents   139
    and Local Businesses

26. Federal and State Governments Collect Taxes   140
    from Residents and Local Businesses

27. Local Governments Purchase Goods and Services   145

28. Local Governments Employ Residents and   146
    Nonresidents

29. A Fish Story – Community Retains Money   148

30. A Fish Story – Community Attracts Money   149

31. A Fish Story – Community Loses Money   151

32. Best Case Business Scenario   157

33. Worst Case Business Scenario   158

Preface

As the past Executive Director of a regional development organization, I've worked with many communities, some prospering, some stagnating and some declining. During regular visits, I would drive around and talk with merchants, business owners and residents. I wanted to figure out what made some communities thrive and flourish and others decline and wither. It took me a while to figure it out, but in the end the answer was simple: prosperous communities generate a positive cash flow. With an ever increasing amount of money to spend, communities prosper. This does not necessarily mean that new businesses are opening, but rather that existing businesses are making a positive contribution to the amount of money in circulation. In other words, a positive cash flow means that the local economy is generating a net increase in the amount of money available for spending.

When I speak with community leaders about creating prosperity, I almost immediately realize that the audience needs a single focus, something that connects economic development to prosperity. Even though many of the individual elements for creating prosperous communities have been around for some time, I've never seen them connected in a comprehensive and meaningful way. In response, I came up with the term "Magnetic Communities" to remind residents, local leaders and economic developers that money must be both attracted and retained to create prosperity. Hopefully, over time, "Magnetic Communities" will be used as a catchphrase for local development strategies that attract and retain money.

As local economic and community development programs evolve to compete in an ever changing global economy, many communities struggle to identify specific strategies they can implement to create and enhance prosperity. There is a lot of talk about creating prosperity, but few new ideas, little action and limited results. *Magnetic Communities* gives residents, local leaders, elected officials and economic developers a clear understanding of what drives their local economy and what real-world strategies they can implement, both individually and as a community, to create and sustain prosperity.

The question comes down to "Why do some communities grow and prosper while others struggle and decline?" Attempts to answer this age old question fill volumes and provide a good living for economic developers, consultants and economists. But, as with most local economic development questions, the answer lies in a basic understanding of how money enters, circulates within, and exits local economies, and not in the economic development strategy du jour.

The economics of prosperity are based on the principle that money, if it is to provide maximum benefits to the local economy, must be both attracted and retained. Similar to a magnet that attracts and retains bits of metal, Magnetic Communities attract and retain money, a process that creates a positive cash flow and establishes the foundation for prosperity.

I cannot count the number of times I've come home from a conference or training session on economic and community development, downtown redevelopment, workforce development, etc. with very little to show for my time, effort and expense. Magnetic Communities do not focus on complicated development models but rather on straight forward strategies implemented by economic and community developers, residents, businesses and governments. While some actions, such as industrial recruitment and tourism development will be familiar to most readers, other actions related to residents, existing businesses and local governments will stimulate new thinking on how communities can achieve prosperity in today's global economy.

Economic and community developers talk about collaborating to compete globally, about creating linkages between key industrial clusters or ecosystems and about signing cooperative agreements to promote regionalism. They go on and on about cultivating creativity, capacity building and local talent to foster an environment conducive to creative ideas and people. They ramble on about advocating for innovation in the workforce, increasing the pool of knowledge-workers and equipping them with higher skills. In short, the economic and community development professions have lost sight of the basic principles that create prosperity. They have created a tangled web of economic development strategies and anointed themselves with professional certifications, elevating the profession, but making it almost impossible for residents and local leaders to participate in the economic and community development process.

In addition, the emergence of a complex global economy has precipitated a greater reliance on professional developers, economists and consultants, creating a disconnect between the economic development process, residents, local businesses and communities in general. Remember, consultants make a living promoting the idea that complex problems require complex solutions, and therefore complex economic development challenges require complex economic development strategies. As a result, communities spend more time, effort and money trying to compete globally, when they should be focused on prospering locally. Rather than relying on regional alliances that seldom benefit all members, it is probably more cost effective and productive to rely on local initiatives to create prosperity. Magnetic Communities work to remove economic development barriers by promoting a greater understanding of the economic development process and by engaging residents, businesses and local governments in the pursuit of community wealth and personal well-being.

Magnetic Communities insure that residents, local businesses and governments understand the specific actions they can take - right now - to promote prosperity. Small actions by many people can make a real impact on prosperity. For example: local businesses filling vacant jobs with qualified residents, manufacturers switching from out-of-town suppliers to local suppliers, residents committing to shop for produce at local farmers markets and local governments committing to hire new employees willing to relocate to the community, all impact local prosperity. It is important to note that Magnetic Communities seek to achieve economic self-determination and not isolation. By creating linkages between local business, residents and governments, Magnetic Communities gain more control over their destiny and future prosperity.

Almost all residents want to live in prosperous communities, and given the opportunity, they are willing to take responsibility for their own economic well-being and to assist their community achieve its economic development goals. Magnetic Communities encourage everyone to get involved in attracting and retaining money and to live a Magnetic Community lifestyle. It takes a community working together to unleash the power of community, not a few economic developers holding confidential project information close to their vest. Magnetic Communities recognize that individuals create prosperity, not communities and governments. Residents must prosper for communities to prosper.

When speaking to community groups about Magnetic Communities, I start by explaining how money enters, circulates within and exits a community. My goal is to show how important it is to not only attract money but also to retain it. Years ago, during the question and answer portion of my presentation, a resident made the following comment and asked a very revealing question. She said, "For all practical purposes, our county-wide economic development program is very successful. We recruited five new manufacturing plants and created over a 1,000 new jobs in the past five years; so why haven't our local businesses and county residents experienced the economic benefits they expected?"

The answer to this question highlights one of the primary reasons I wrote *Magnetic Communities*. When communities announce the location of new businesses and the creation of new jobs, the public assumes that these businesses will employ local workers and purchase local materials, supplies and services. In reality though, many new companies use existing supplier networks and hire workers who commute from surrounding communities.

Take the example of a heavy equipment assembly plant. The relocating company negotiates free land and tax rebates for the first 10 years. When several local contractors win bids to help build the new facility, everyone in the community is feeling good about the project. Two years later an analysis of the project shows that parts for assembly are steadily being shipped to the new facility and finished goods are being shipped to customers worldwide. But because parts are sourced overseas and from other plants in the US, local manufactures are not benefitting from the new assembly plant. The community, which expected an economic boost from the 100 new jobs, is disappointed to find that 60 of the 100 employees, including top managers, chose to live in neighboring counties where housing is readily available, newer and located in better school districts. Once the plant is up and running, the community discovers that contracts for office supplies, technology, maintenance requirements and a host of other services are being filled through existing agreements negotiated with the company's headquarters located in another state.

In my experience, the preceding example is more often the rule than the exception. Economic developers, and I include myself, work to relocate new businesses and to create new jobs regardless if they maximize local benefits. Once the initial announcement is made and ground is broken, economic developers, elected officials and community leaders are off working on the next project, leaving the most important part of the current project to take care of itself. With just a little forethought and planning, the economic impact of many relocation and expansion projects can easily be doubled. I place the preceding example in the category of "same old/ same old" where long-time leaders focus on what they know worked in the past and not on what works in today's technology-based global market place.

Communities seeking to prosper locally in the global economy must make better use of the money and resources close at hand. To this end, Magnetic Communities must focus their economic and community development efforts on attracting and retaining money, two strategies that generate and sustain a positive cash flow and prosperity. In other words, even though money is considered attracted when a new business announcement is made, money is not retained until new jobs are filled by residents and contracts for services and supplies are awarded to local businesses. Money must be both attracted and retained!

Introduction

Magnetic Communities include towns, cities, counties, states and regions that excel in attracting and retaining money, a process that creates a positive cash flow. Because local businesses, residents and local governments have an ever increasing amount of money to spend, they prosper. Prosperity allows businesses to grow, create jobs and pay dividends; it allows residents to improve their personal well-being by providing the money necessary for better housing, healthcare, education, leisure activities, etc.; and it allows governments to generate the tax revenue necessary to provide the services residents and businesses need to succeed.

When someone asks me where I live, I say New Bern, North Carolina. I consider myself part of the New Bern community and its economy. But because my residence is physically located outside the city limits in Craven County, I am subject to the laws and regulations that govern the County and not the City. My local jurisdiction is Craven County.

In reality, people pay little attention to whether they live, work, and shop inside or outside a particular jurisdiction. Occasionally, they are reminded of where they are by a sign welcoming them to so-and-so county or city, or when they get their property tax bill from the county, city or both. They may also be reminded of where they are when they get a traffic ticket from the city police, county sheriff or state trooper.

The term *local jurisdiction* refers to an incorporated village, town, city, county or group of local jurisdictions acting as a region. This distinction is important because many local jurisdictions fund economic and community development efforts that are intended to benefit residents of the jurisdiction. When the city council provides funding for an economic development project, the city is interested in creating jobs and in increasing the tax base to support government activities and services for residents and businesses of the jurisdiction. If the city's economic development funds are used to locate a new business just outside the city limits, city residents have access to the new jobs but the county, not the city, will benefit from the capital investment and tax revenue. For city residents to benefit fully from the city's investment in economic development, the new business must locate within the city limits, where the city will also benefit from the capital investment.

As the world's markets become increasingly global, it becomes more and more difficult for small towns and counties to compete. To offset this growing disadvantage, local jurisdictions have found it effective to form regional partnerships. Because regional partnerships are usually made up of groups of local jurisdictions, they operate a lot like individual jurisdictions.

Communities and local economies are made up of individuals and groups of individuals that interact with each other regularly within their immediate surroundings. A typical community consists of residents, businesses and governments that interact to provide social, commercial, and regulatory activities. Within a community, the network of businesses and consumers makes up the local economy. For purposes of this book, the terms local jurisdiction, community and local economy are used interchangeably. Even though the terms community and local economy are broader than a local jurisdiction and do not have distinct boundaries, they all include groups of interrelated businesses, residents and governments.

As will become evident, strategies for creating prosperous communities are based on attracting and retaining new money. The term "new money" is used when referring to money that enters a local economy. For example, new money enters a community when tourists purchase local goods, when retirees receive Social Security checks and when local manufacturers sell products outside the local economy. New money is retained when it is spent locally.

The terms "attract" and "retain" are commonly used by economic developers in connection with businesses, jobs and investments, as in "The community's goal is to attract and retain manufacturing firms." When used in the context of *Magnetic Communities,* the terms refer to money, as in "Magnetic Communities seek to attract and retain money."

Even though Magnetic Community principles hold true for both large and small communities, many of the examples in *Magnetic Communities* are for smaller communities and businesses where concepts and principles are easier to describe and understand.

Magnetic Community strategies compliment, rather than replace, traditional economic and community development strategies. The broader discussion of economic and community development strategies, as they apply to Magnetic

Communities, is discussed in Chapter 5, Community Strategies. Chapters 6 – 10 discuss Magnetic Community strategies for businesses, tourists, residents, retirees and local governments respectively. Because every community has a unique set of assets and liabilities, a general understanding of Magnetic Community strategies and how they work allows communities to develop and implement generalized strategies applicable to almost all communities or to develop individualized strategies for specific needs.

To illustrate how money enters, circulates within and exits a community, *Magnetic Communities* contains numerous illustrations built on a common representation of the global and local economies (Illustration 1, page 6). The area inside the large circle represents the local economy and everything outside the large circle represents the global economy. Smaller circles located inside and outside the local economy are labeled to designate their role in the money flow process (e.g. businesses, residents, nonresidents, customers, etc.). Labeled arrows show the flow of money, goods, services and labor between businesses, residents, governments, etc. When arrows show money flowing from the global economy into the local economy, money is being attracted (Illustration 1). When arrows show money circulating within the local economy, money is being retained (Illustration 2, page 7). When arrows show money flowing out of the local economy into the global economy, money is being lost. Even though sales taxes are part of almost all transactions, illustrations do not track them. The intent of the illustrations is to help readers visualize the general flow of money and not to track every penny. Illustrations depict transactions that attract and retain money. They do not show the impact of economic multipliers (Chapter 4, page 41).

From a Magnetic Community perspective, prosperity means community wealth and personal well-being. Community wealth includes the value of a community's tangible assets such as cash, land, buildings, equipment, infrastructure, etc. and intangible assets such as leadership, social networks, knowledge, reputation, quality of life, etc. Personal well-being represents the level of health, happiness, and financial success of a community's residents.

Understanding the Economics of Prosperity starts with an understanding of how money flows through the community. Money starts flowing when it is spent. As money flows between businesses, tourists, individuals, retirees and governments, it leaves a trail of benefits and missed opportunities.

Illustration 1

Nonresidents Purchase Goods and Services from Local Businesses

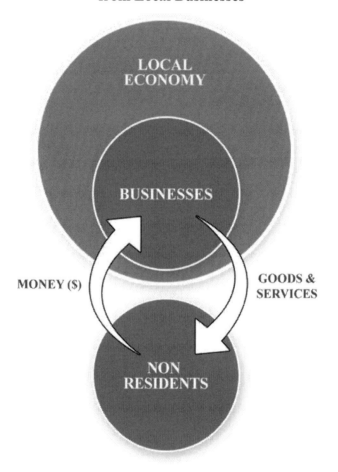

When nonresidents (tourists, visitors, etc.) spend money purchasing goods and services from local businesses, money flows into the local economy and to local businesses. Because the local economy and local businesses have more money to spend they prosper.

Illustration 2

**Residents Purchase Goods and Services
from Local Businesses**

When residents spend money purchasing goods and services from local businesses, local businesses make money and money already in circulation is retained, but because the entire transaction takes place inside the local economy, new money is not attracted to the community.

By examining the money trail, communities can evaluate their effectiveness in attracting and retaining money as it works its way through the community. Attracting new money is vital to the goal of creating prosperity. New money replaces money lost to spending outside the local economy and adds to the money already in circulation. With more money in circulation for longer periods of time, the benefits of local spending are multiplied (See Chapter 4, Multipliers).

So, what can individuals do to create prosperity? In today's global economy, individuals, not communities and governments, create prosperity. This may seem counter intuitive; but in the global marketplace, communities are competing less and less with each other for jobs and investments, but rather, individuals are competing directly with each other for jobs. In today's job environment, where an individual's physical location is less and less important, the bottom line becomes the individual's skill set and ability to communicate, making the starting point for prosperity the individual, not incentives offered to companies by communities and governments. Location and quality of life issues remain important but more so for individuals and less so for businesses. Many of today's job seekers look for a place to live before they look for a place to work or start a business.

Magnetic Communities examines how the flow of money impacts the economic success and prosperity of a community and how businesses, residents and governments, along with economic developers and community leaders, can identify and implement strategies that create and enhance local prosperity. Rather than a broad set of vague high level strategies that no one really understands or knows how to implement, Magnetic

Communities base strategies on straight forward real world actions by businesses, residents, retirees and local governments that attract and retain money. For example, where people work, where they live and where they spend are not just interesting demographics, they are critical factors that represent the difference between prosperity and hardship.

Part One

Economics of Prosperity

Magnetic Community Strategies and traditional economic development have many of the same measures of success. For example, the unemployment rate, median household income and the total value of an area's tax base remain important; but Magnetic Communities also measure attributes such as home ownership, education, savings, health, income and safety to name a few, all of which are wrapped up in the term, quality of life.

Many residents read about local efforts to recruit new businesses, jobs and investments but do not fully understand how the local economy works. When asked what they expect from their community's economic development efforts, residents say more jobs, more places to shop, more residential construction, more economic growth, etc. When questioned further though, most residents realize what they really want is prosperity, or a better quality of life.

Magnetic Communities prosper by implementing strategies that create a positive cash flow. In other words, more money is flowing into a community than is flowing out. For example, when a local manufacturer makes a product and sells it outside the local economy, new money flows into the community in the form of wages. If workers live and spend locally, new money is retained and available for additional spending; if workers live and spend outside the local economy, money flows out of the community and there is little or no local benefit. Also, when a tourist spends money at a local business, new money flows into the community. If the tourism business is locally owned, hires local workers, and purchases local materials, supplies and services, money stays in the community and is available for further spending; if not, there is little local benefit beyond the tourist's original purchase. By following the money trail, communities can evaluate whether or not the local economy is attracting and retaining enough money to create a positive cash flow. Anything communities can do to improve the cash flow equation is a move towards achieving prosperity.

Historically, a workforce growing in both size and quality fueled prosperity; baby boomers and women entered the workforce as college graduation rates increased. Today, baby boomers are retiring, women are a stable part of the workforce and college graduation rates have leveled off. In the past, cities and regions developed industrial parks and offered incentive packages to entice companies to locate operations in their community. In a static industrial-based economy, this kind of traditional economic development is effective. Looking to the future though, is this tactical approach going to provide the jobs and local investment needed for communities to prosper locally in a global economy?

Traditional economic and community development efforts measure success primarily by the number of new jobs and capital investment; when in reality, individuals, communities and governments would be better off measuring the success of their development efforts by focusing on prosperity. For instance, if a business announces a new $20 million manufacturing plant with 200 jobs, community leaders need to ask the question, "Will residents, existing businesses and local governments be better off?" If measured by the number of new jobs and capital investment, the answer may be yes. If measured by prosperity - community wealth and personal well-being - the answer may be something very different.

While most community and government leaders want to improve levels of prosperity, many of their efforts and investments are misguided. Take the previous example of a $20 million manufacturing plant with 200 new jobs. If the new plant strains the community's existing water and sewer system, negatively impacts the natural environment and was won with tax incentives, the community may not experience any prosperity improvements at all. Likewise, if some or most of the jobs are less than full time, have low skill requirements, pay below average wages and do not include health insurance, employees may find themselves working, but no more prosperous. It is true that unskilled workers and new workforce entrants with little education and skill will benefit from almost any job opportunity; but will these job opportunities create the prosperity communities and governments seek? This is not to suggest that communities and governments abandon traditional economic development efforts, but rather that they expand their awareness and measure of success to include prosperity.

A successful economic development program does not

guarantee prosperity. As illustrated above, when the local headline reads "New industry plans to invest $20 million and create 200 new jobs," there are a lot of questions that need to be asked and answered before residents can determine the project's economic benefit to the community. It's not complicated, but just like businesses and individuals; communities prosper when they generate a positive cash flow. It's not all about the money, but as with most things, money plays an important role in the creation of prosperous communities.

In the final analysis, communities and governments cannot create prosperity. Residents must prosper for communities to prosper, and communities must prosper for governments to prosper. The obvious approach then is to implement economic development strategies that create prosperous residents. Just think about it, when was the last time you saw a prosperous community without prosperous residents.

One of the reasons individual residents get lost in the economic development process is because they are lumped together into groups such as plant managers, educators, school administrators, blue collar workers, elected officials, retirees, etc., which takes away from their individuality as members of the community. Each of the groups mentioned above is made up of individuals with names like John, Ann, Jim, etc. These individuals have multiple roles to play. For example, a local plant manager has a role as a business leader and as a resident.

To facilitate the discussion of Magnetic Communities, strategies have been divided into five groups; they include: businesses, tourists, residents, retirees and local governments.

Each group plays a role in the flow of money, but most importantly each group is made up of individuals, many of whom influence how money is spent. Even though companies and governments may have purchasing polices, let's not forget that individuals establish policies, and when everything is said and done, individuals make purchasing decisions, not companies.

When the community newspaper reports that the local lumber mill is closing, it's not the lumber mill that decided to close, it's "Bob" the plant manager and his seven-member board of directors that decided to close the mill. Likewise, the resident-owner of a local business can make personal purchases in her role as a resident or business purchases in her role as a business owner. In both cases, an individual made the purchasing decision, not an individual and a business.

In the past, recruiting and retaining good paying manufacturing jobs was the best strategy for creating prosperous communities. Today's strategies must also target education, workforce development, entrepreneurship, innovation and quality of life to mention a few. Magnetic Communities not only seek to attract businesses with good paying jobs, but also tourists, retirees and residents looking for an exceptional quality of life. All of which can be accomplished by keeping the community's economic development strategies focused on the flow of money, individual involvement and on attracting and retaining money.

CHAPTER ONE

Money Flow

Economic development is the process of improving the economic health, quality of life, and prosperity of a community. In the process, economic developers, elected officials, community leaders and residents must make critical decisions about allocating limited resources and about prioritizing development strategies to maximize outcomes. *Magnetic Communities* explains how communities can achieve prosperity by applying money flow principles to develop and implement economic development strategies.

When I look around my community I see residents going to work, manufacturers shipping goods, businesses providing services, local merchants stocking shelves, tourists enjoying lunch, retirees taking a walk, newcomers building homes, entrepreneurs starting businesses, city employees setting up for a parade, etc. All of these activities set the stage and create a flow of money that determines a community's prosperity. If these activities create a net increase in the amount of money available for spending, the local economy grows and prospers. On the other hand, if these activities create a net decrease in the amount of money available for spending, the local economy shrinks and languishes. Can it be any simpler and clearer than that?!

Money Flow Examples:

The following three money flow examples depict a community with steady increases in the inflow of money. What changes in each of the three examples is the amount of money flowing out of the local economy. This is an important principle. Most communities are able to identify where money enters the community but fail to recognize where money exits. Money outflows must be kept to a minimum if a community is to create a positive cash flow and prosper.

Of course there are many more iterations of the following line and bar charts. From my experience, the three scenarios depicted here are the most prevalent and set the stage for readers to develop their own money flow graphics.

Illustration 3

Money Flow – Stable local economy

The dark gray line, in the following line charts, represents the inflow of money over eight years. Money is steadily flowing into the local economy and increasing over time. During the eight years, the inflow of money increases from $10 million to $15.25 million. The parallel light gray line represents the outflow of money, which increases from $4 million to $9.25 million over the same period. The important thing to note is that both the inflow and outflow have increased $5.25 million, while the amount of money in circulation and available for spending, represented by the distance between the two gray lines, remains constant at $6 million. Residents of the community may look around and feel like the community is growing and better off, but in reality the money available for spending remains constant.

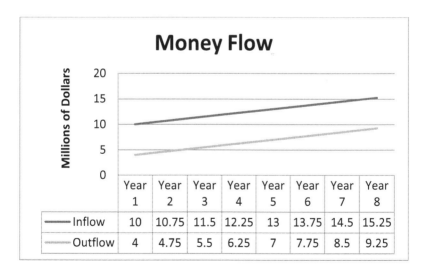

	Year 1	Year 2	Year 3	Year 4	Year 5	Year 6	Year 7	Year 8
Inflow	10	10.75	11.5	12.25	13	13.75	14.5	15.25
Outflow	4	4.75	5.5	6.25	7	7.75	8.5	9.25

By converting the Illustration 3 line chart into a bar chart, it is easier to see that the amount of money available for spending remains constant as the inflow and outflow increase. The medium gray bar on the bar chart clearly shows that the amount of money *available for spending remains constant at $6.0 million over the eight years.*

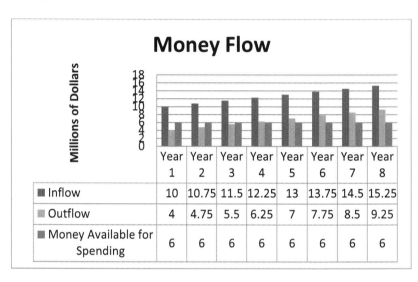

The community depicted in Illustration 3 is growing and attracting an increasing amount of money to the local economy. At the same time, the rate at which money is flowing out of the local economy is increasing proportionately. Even though the community may look and feel like it is prospering (more businesses, more residents, etc.) it is stagnating. Because communities have more control over outflows than inflows of money, the most effective way to improve a community's prosperity is to retain additional money, thereby increasing the amount of money in circulation and available for spending. If an outflow cannot be stopped, Magnetic Communities attempt to reduce its impact on the local economy. The Magnetic Community Strategies section (Chapters 5 – 10) specifically address how to increase inflows and decrease outflows, or how to attract and retain money.

Illustration 4

Money Flow – Growing Local Economy

Again, the dark gray line in the line chart represents the inflow of money over the same eight-year time period and is identical to Illustration 3. In Illustration 4, the steady growth of money flowing into the community is accompanied by a slower increase of money flowing out. More money is being retained. This slower increase may be the result of local businesses employing more residents and purchasing more goods and services locally. In addition, residents may be spending more money locally. Overall, the amount of money available for spending is increasing over time, providing the community with a positive cash flow.

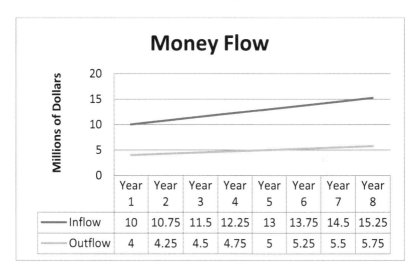

	Year 1	Year 2	Year 3	Year 4	Year 5	Year 6	Year 7	Year 8
Inflow	10	10.75	11.5	12.25	13	13.75	14.5	15.25
Outflow	4	4.25	4.5	4.75	5	5.25	5.5	5.75

Once more, by converting the Illustration 4 line chart into a bar chart, it is easier to see that the amount of money available for spending is increasing. The medium gray bar on the bar chart shows that the amount of money available for spending increases from $6.0 million to $9.5 million over eight years.

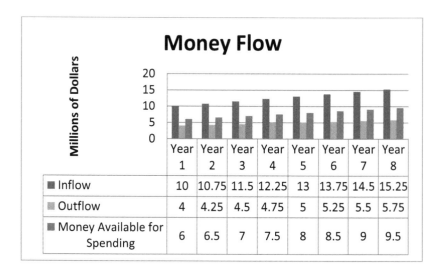

Money Flow

Millions of Dollars

	Year 1	Year 2	Year 3	Year 4	Year 5	Year 6	Year 7	Year 8
▪ Inflow	10	10.75	11.5	12.25	13	13.75	14.5	15.25
▪ Outflow	4	4.25	4.5	4.75	5	5.25	5.5	5.75
▪ Money Available for Spending	6	6.5	7	7.5	8	8.5	9	9.5

Illustration 4 is the Magnetic Community model. By keeping the inflow of money steadily increasing and by decreasing the rate at which money is flowing out of the community, the community creates a positive cash flow and increases both the amount of money available for spending and local prosperity.

Illustration 5

Money Flow – Shrinking Local Economy

The dark gray line in the line chart in Illustration 5 represents the flow of money into the community and is identical to the first two illustrations. It increases steadily over eight years from $10 million to $15.25 million, or $5.25 million. The light gray line represents the flow of money out of the community. It increases steadily over the eight-year period from $4 million to $12.75 million, or $8.75 million. Because money is flowing out of the local economy at a rate faster than it is flowing in, there is a net outflow and less money in circulation for spending.

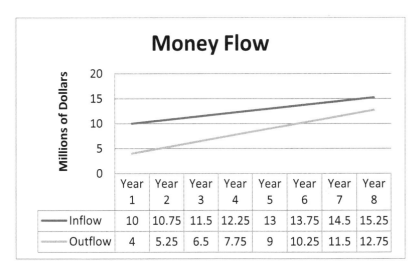

	Year 1	Year 2	Year 3	Year 4	Year 5	Year 6	Year 7	Year 8
Inflow	10	10.75	11.5	12.25	13	13.75	14.5	15.25
Outflow	4	5.25	6.5	7.75	9	10.25	11.5	12.75

By looking at the related bar chart for Illustration 5, it is evident that the outflow of money is growing faster than the inflow. As a result, the money available for spending is shrinking.

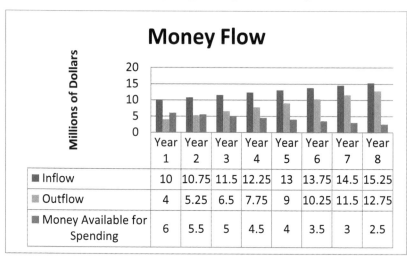

Money Flow

Millions of Dollars

	Year 1	Year 2	Year 3	Year 4	Year 5	Year 6	Year 7	Year 8
■ Inflow	10	10.75	11.5	12.25	13	13.75	14.5	15.25
■ Outflow	4	5.25	6.5	7.75	9	10.25	11.5	12.75
■ Money Available for Spending	6	5.5	5	4.5	4	3.5	3	2.5

Identical to Illustrations 3 and 4, the community in Illustration 5 is attracting more money over the eight-year period. At the same time though, the rate at which money is flowing out of the local economy is increasing even faster. Once the amount of money available for spending starts shrinking and there is less and less money in circulation, businesses stop growing and start closing. With fewer local stores and businesses open to provide materials, supplies and services, local businesses and residents must resort to making purchases outside the local economy. Outside spending further increases the outflow of money. It takes a long time and a concerted effort to turn local economies around, but it can be accomplished by implementing Magnetic Community strategies that attract and retain money.

The idea of developing money flow strategies first came to me early in my career. It was my second week on the job as the County's economic developer and I was going around introducing myself to the plant managers. During one of the meetings, I asked a recently transferred manager if he was happy with the housing choices in the County. He hesitated for a moment and said that housing was something I needed to look into because he and almost all of his management team lived in the two neighboring counties. After a few more questions and further discussion, I realized that many of the production workers also lived outside of the County. As a result, money flowed into the County in the form of wages and flowed right back out when employees spent their paychecks in neighboring counties. This attitude that everything was better outside the County also carried over into the company's purchase of materials, supplies and services, which deprived local businesses of potential income and the community of the prosperity it was looking to achieve.

As individuals go about their daily lives and businesses work to make a profit, money flows from business to business, individual to individual, and between businesses and individuals. Money also flows within and between towns, cities, counties, regions, states and countries. As a result, some individuals, businesses and communities generate a positive cash flow and prosper, while others do not. There are winners and losers!

It is important to understand how money flow works and how it impacts prosperity. Money flowing into a community not only replaces money that leaks out, it is also the source of new money that funds economic growth and prosperity. On the down side, if money is not flowing into a community as fast as it is flowing out, the local economy will decline in both vitality and size. As one might expect, Magnetic Communities are focused on two money flow goals: (1) increasing inflows and

(2) decreasing outflows. Communities increase inflows by attracting money to the local economy and decrease outflows by increasing the time money circulates locally and by stopping money from flowing out of the local economy. Both of these money flow goals are encompassed in the Magnetic Community strategies of attracting and retaining money.

To become a Magnetic Community, communities must evaluate their local economy for potential sources of new money and ways it can be retained. They must also look for ways to improve the money flow ratio (inflow to outflow) by gathering information and by determining how money enters, circulates within and exits the community. Money flow principles also help communities evaluate existing economic development efforts and returns on investment. In many cases, the problem is not that too little money flows into the local economy, but rather that residents, businesses and public agencies spend too much money outside the local economy. For example, if community residents regularly run into each other at an outlet mall in a neighboring county, money is probably flowing out of the community. The Magnetic Community strategy is not to locate a competing outlet mall in their community, but rather to buy locally when possible and increase purchases of products and services that are available locally. If dressier clothes are not available locally, go to the outlet mall; but if locally available fishing and hunting gear, work cloths, garden supplies, furniture, appliances, tools, farm equipment and fresh produce are priced competitively in local stores; stay in town to purchase these items.

Sometimes, when trying to explain what something is, it is helpful to look at what something is not. Many communities have become blind to the fact that their local economy is in trouble. The good news is that less prosperous communities can use Magnetic Community strategies to turn things around. In fact, the positive impact of Magnetic Community strategies is more pronounced in poorer communities than in those that are better off.

You may not live in a Magnetic Community if:

- Most local businesses sell products and services to each other and to residents
- Many local businesses are headquartered elsewhere
- There are few professional and manufacturing jobs
- The local economy consists of low paying service and retail sector jobs
- Business closures are a regular event
- Tourism is almost nonexistent
- Hotels are older, low-end independent operations
- There are few, if any, bed and breakfasts
- Few businesses are expanding
- Few new businesses are being started
- Many local workers choose to live outside the community (including local government workers)
- Many residents shop in surrounding communities
- Many residents move out of the community to retire

Specific money flow strategies for businesses, tourists, residents, retirees and local governments are discussed in Chapters 6 – 10 and include illustrations to help readers visualize the flow of money as it creates a money trail through the local economy. In general, money flow impacts a community in three different ways.

1. Money flows into a community when:

- Local businesses sell goods and services outside the local economy
- Residents work outside the community or are paid from outside sources
- Tourists and visitors (nonresidents) spend money locally
- Retirees receive money from Social Security, pensions and outside savings
- Governments receive tax payments and other revenue from outside the jurisdiction

2. Money circulates in a community when:

- Local businesses and governments purchase raw materials, supplies and services locally
- Local businesses and governments employ residents
- Residents spend locally

3. Money flows out of a community when:

- Local businesses and governments purchase materials, supplies and services outside the local economy
- Local businesses and governments employ non residents
- Local businesses are not locally owned and operated
- Residents purchase goods and services outside the local economy

CHAPTER TWO

Money Trail

Similar to an investigative reporter, economic developers and community leaders can determine who is benefiting from local transactions by following the money. If the motivation behind local economic development efforts is to create prosperity, it is crucial to understand how the money trail winds its way through the community.

A Money Trail begins when money enters the local economy and ends when it exits. Think of money trails as the roads that lead into town, circulate traffic within the town and lead back out. The amount of time money circulates, the number of times it changes hands and the path it follows has a profound effect on how much benefit it provides local residents, businesses and governments.

Once in the local economy, money can follow many different paths. By identifying both existing and potential sources of money, communities can make strategic decisions to protect and grow existing inflows while targeting new sources of money for development. For example, a community's money trail for tourism may begin when travelers exit the interstate and travel downtown. Visitors may then spend time in the commercial area before moving on to the museum district, and finally to the chain restaurants on the bypass before heading down the road. To keep tourists spending longer in the local economy, communities may consider assisting a local entrepreneur start a restaurant down town, establish a bed and breakfast or recruit a hotel to the bypass. By extending the money trail to include more places to eat, stay and spend, Magnetic Communities seek to attract more money and to retain it longer. As a side benefit, improvements to a community's tourism infrastructure, such as restaurants, cultural amenities and places to stay, also include the kind of amenities residents and retirees are looking for in a place to live.

Individuals are free to live, work and spend wherever they want, inside or outside the local economy. Likewise, businesses and governments are free to hire employees, purchase goods and contract for services from inside or outside the local economy. This free flowing economic structure allows money a wide range of movement. It also sets the stage for aggressive economic development efforts aimed at directing and redirecting money along the money trail to benefit local economic interests. As a result, competitive economic development efforts pit towns, cities, counties, regions, states and countries against one another. As mentioned previously, it also produces winners and losers, which explains why some communities are more prosperous than others. But, in many cases winners are no better off than losers. By following the money trail it is possible to show why and how economic development efforts positively or negatively impact development outcomes and a community's overall prosperity.

The length of time money stays in circulation, the number of times it changes hands and the path it follows, greatly impacts how much benefit it provides local residents, businesses and governments. Magnetic Communities recognize that new money entering the community creates a trail of benefits and missed opportunities as it works its way through the local economy. In response, Magnetic Communities identify, develop and implement strategies that maximize the economic benefits and minimize missed opportunities, thereby maximizing prosperity.

A typical money trail may include a tourist's purchase of a pottery vase from a local artist, the subsequent purchase by the artist of a hamburger for lunch at a local restaurant, the purchase of beef from a local farmer by the restaurant owner and the purchase of a plane ticket by the farmer to visit his son. In this example, money enters the local economy when the tourist purchases the pottery vase. The new money circulates locally when the artist buys lunch and the restaurant owner purchases beef. It exits the local economy when the farmer purchases a plane ticket to visit his son.

Now consider the same tourist's purchase of a vase; but this time rather than buying lunch locally, the artist realizes she is low on art supplies and decides to grab lunch in a neighboring town where the art supply store is located. In this case, both the money spent on art supplies and lunch represent outflows from the local economy. As a result, the local restaurant and farmer do not benefit from the original expenditure by the tourist. The artist may have no choice about where to purchase art supplies, but if she is aware that lunch purchased locally helps her community prosper she may drive back to town and have lunch with friends.

Following the money trail helps local leaders determine how much benefit money provides the local economy as it travels through the community. Once in the local economy, communities must develop strategies to circulate money locally. This insures that money is retained as long as possible, maximizing its potential benefit. Finally, communities must do everything they can to keep money from flowing out of the local economy. Money lost to outside spending is no longer available to provide economic benefits.

A good place to start identifying and following a money trail is with local government. Budget and financial data are accessible and available to the public. Start with the municipality's largest source of revenue and determine if it originates inside or outside the local jurisdiction. For example, tax revenue from levies on real estate and personal property are almost always generated locally and do not represent new money for the local economy. Exceptions such as a branch manufacturing plant, a regional electric generating facility, commercial and residential investment property, etc., should be noted and prioritized by the community for retention and expansion potential. More details and information on creating and enhancing local government money trails are discussed in Chapter 10, Government Strategies.

CHAPTER THREE

New Money

Even though Magnetic Communities seek to attract and retain money, attracting money remains the top priority. New money is king because communities cannot retain and circulate what they do not have. All communities lose money over time to such things as vacations, new cars, utilities, state and Federal taxes, etc. New money not only replaces money that leaks out of every economy; it is also the source of economic growth and prosperity.

When a husband and wife both work, they are both generating new money for the family. If the children receive an allowance for completing chores around the house, they receive a portion of the parent's new money. The allowance is new money to the children but the family as a whole has no additional money to spend. On the other hand, if the parents do not believe in paying allowances for work around the house and the children still want their own money to spend, they may choose to babysit the neighbor's children. In this case, not only have the children generated new money for themselves, but they have also generated new money for the family, improving the family's overall prosperity. The same principle holds true for communities. For example, when I walk up the street to the local coffee shop and buy a cup of coffee, the coffee shop has more money; but because I live locally, the community has no additional money. On the other hand, if an out of town salesman or a tourist purchases a cup of coffee, both the coffee shop and the community have more money to spend. It is important to know the difference between spending that attracts new money and spending that circulates money already in the community. Understanding the significance of these two very similar but different transactions is one of the keys to understanding why new money is king and why Magnetic Communities prosper.

Not all money is created equal. A paycheck earned by a local manufacturing employee is more valuable than an equal paycheck earned by, let's say, a local government employee. The manufacturing employee helps produce a product that is sold outside the local economy; the government employee provides a service to local residents. Because manufactured products are sold and paid for with money from outside the local economy, new money flows back to the plant and to its employees as wages. On the other hand, local government employees are paid from taxes collected from residents. This keeps money in circulation locally but produces no new money for the economy. The issue of value is not one of a manufacturing job versus a service job but rather where the money to pay the two employees comes from, inside or outside the local economy (Illustrations 6 & 7, pages 36 & 37).

In addition, new money earned by local businesses and residents is not necessarily new money for the community. When a local customer pays a local machine shop for a completed job, the machine shop has more money to spend but the community does not. This also holds true for individuals who live and work locally. A resident's paycheck from a local employer is new money for the resident but not for the community. In both cases money is retained and circulated but no new money is generated; for that to happen, companies and/or sources from outside the community must pay the machine shop and the local employee.

Increasing the inflow of new money is exactly why industrial recruitment continues to be a top economic development strategy. When a local manufacturer makes a product and sells it outside the local economy, proceeds from the sale generate the revenue necessary to pay production costs, worker salaries and investors. If a manufacturing facility in North Carolina produces a dishwasher that is sold to a home builder in California, money from the sale flows back to North Carolina. The money will be used to pay workers, parts suppliers, stockholders, utilities, property taxes, insurance, transportation, etc. Even if the parts suppliers, stockholders, utility companies, insurance firms, and transportation providers are not part of the local economy where the dishwasher was made, the manufacturing plant and workers are, which means that property taxes and wages will generate new money for the local economy.

Illustration 6

The Value of Manufacturing Wages

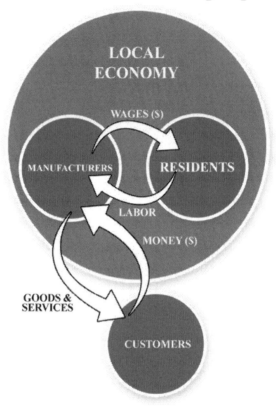

In this traditional economic development example, local manufacturers sell goods and services to customers outside the local economy. New money is attracted when goods and services are sold, and retained when resident workers are paid. Because wages are generated from the sale of goods and services sold outside the local economy they contribute to the Magnetic Community goal of creating a positive cash flow. Both manufacturers and the community are better off. Later illustrations and discussions show the flow of money when workers are not residents.

Illustration 7

The Value of Local Government Wages

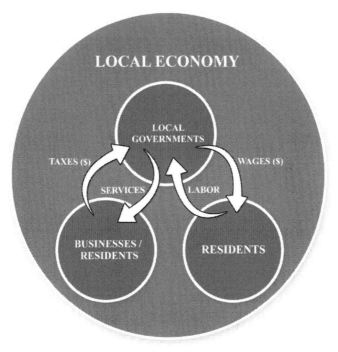

To provide services and to pay resident-employees, local governments collect taxes from local businesses and residents. Money is retained but new money is not attracted. Even if the paychecks in Illustrations 6 and 7 are for the same amount, the economic impact of government checks are less because they are generated from local tax dollars already in circulation. In this illustration, resident-employees have more money to spend but the local economy is no better off.

Just because new money is king is no reason to focus entirely on attracting money. Many communities with traditional economic and community development programs fall into this trap. They declare success every time a new plant or business is announced. They take the attitude that once money is attracted, the rest will take care of itself.

Most community businesses are consumer-based. They include retail stores, plumbers, lawn care services, restaurants, banks, lawyers, doctors, etc. These businesses do not generally attract new money but rather retain and circulate money already in the local economy. Local spending benefits from the multiplier effect (see Chapter 4) and potentially impacts prosperity even more than new money. But again, when all is said and done, money has to be attracted and retained before it can produce economic multipliers.

When identifying sources of new money, it is important to identify all major sources, both existing and potential. For example, even though the military, tourism and retirees are major new money sources for the community where I live in eastern North Carolina, agriculture, forestry and fishing continue to be substantial contributors to the local economy. Also, about an hour north of where I live is Greenville, NC and East Carolina University. With approximately 30,000 students, the new money generated from tuition payments and other sources of money are substantial. The potential for Greenville and surrounding towns to capitalize on the university's economic engine is substantial.

Communities that prioritize sources of new money by their contribution to the local economy maximize the impact of their new money potential. I have always advocated for a comprehensive approach to economic development, so even though most of a community's new money may be generated from tourism, do not ignore the farmers on the outskirts of town selling fresh fruits, vegetables and flowers to tourists as they come and go.

CHAPTER FOUR

Multipliers

It is important to know what economic multipliers are and how they affect the flow of money. When new money enters the local economy it can be re-spent many times or exit quickly. As new money circulates in the local economy, spending increases above the original amount, "multiplying" its total economic benefit. Less important to the discussion of Magnetic Communities is the actual value of the multiplier itself. Knowing that local spending retains money in the local economy and that this money is multiplying in value should be enough to focus economic development strategies on attracting and retaining money.

Magnetic Communities use economic multipliers to estimate and to measure the total economic impact of local spending.

Because money re-spent by members of the community has the same economic impact as attracting and spending new money, it is helpful to have a shortcut that estimates the total amount of spending.

A local economic multiplier is a number (usually between one and three) that helps determine the total economic impact a community can expect from a change in the local economy. For example, if a local manufacturing facility signs a new contract with an out of town customer, increasing potential income, the local economic impact can be determined by multiplying the increase in income (new money) by the local multiplier. Likewise, if the manufacturer loses a contract to an outside competitor, the negative economic impact can be determined by multiplying the loss by the local multiplier.

Multipliers are computed by dividing the total change in spending by the initial change. For instance, if one new dollar is attracted to a community and each time it is re-spent 50% is retained and 50% is lost to outside spending, the multiplier is computed by dividing the total change in spending by the initial change: ($1 + $.50 + $.25 + $.125 + $.0625)/$1 = 1.9375. In this example, the multiplier, after five rounds of spending is 1.9. It is not just the first round of spending that is important, subsequent rounds are smaller but continue to increase the total economic impact.

Multipliers are an important aspect of all economic development programs. With their focus on retaining money in pursuit of prosperity, it is especially important to Magnetic Communities. Despite their importance, multipliers work in the background and many times are not credited with the important role they play. The discussion and value of multipliers are often hidden in the appendices. In addition, multipliers are based on approximations, estimates and industry averages, making them suspect and difficult to prove. Getting a multiplier from a reputable source, such as the U.S. Commerce Department's Bureau of Economic Analysis (BEA) adds credibility to economic impact calculations.

Not all multipliers measure the same thing. They can measure sales, employment, income and value added. Within these general categories, multipliers are further broken down by direct, indirect and induced effects. Because Magnetic Communities are interested in attracting and retaining money, the focus is on sales and the sub categories of direct, indirect and induced effects. When a local company expands production to fill orders from outside the local economy, additional sales revenue eventually flows back into the community. Expanded production requires additional spending on labor, materials, transportation services and utilities. The additional spending required to produce the product is a direct multiplier effect. In turn, local suppliers will also have to increase spending to fulfill larger contracts. The additional spending by suppliers is an indirect multiplier effect. When money from increased spending by the manufacturer and its suppliers reaches employees and households, the additional money they spend locally is an induced multiplier effect.

Multipliers can be used for planning or for estimating the total economic impact of changes to the local economy. Knowing that higher multipliers mean greater economic impact, allows planners to invest time and money more effectively. Because multipliers increase when local spending increases, creating local linkages and supply chains for parts and services is an important Magnetic Community strategy.

If a local manufacturer makes a $10,000 product and sells it to a customer in another state, proceeds from the sale flow back to the manufacturer and to the community, generating a $10,000 economic benefit. As long as the proceeds from the original transaction continue to circulate locally they provide additional benefits. To expand this example further, let's say the manufacturer spends half of the proceeds ($5,000) on local supplies, services and wages, and the other half to purchase parts from suppliers in other states. The half spent locally continues to provide local economic benefits, while the economic benefits from the money spent in other states is enjoyed by other communities. Let's also say that employees and local vendors spend half of what they receive on daycare, lawn services, fresh produce and eating out at local restaurants, and the other half outside the local economy on things like utilities, mortgages, and car payments. Again, half of the $5,000 ($2,500) stays in the local economy. The multiplier for this example after three rounds of spending is calculated by adding the original sale ($10,000) to the amount paid for local salaries, services and supplies ($5,000) and the amount spent locally on goods and services ($2,500). This sum is then divided by the original sale ($10,000 + $5,000 + $2,500/ $10,000) for a multiplier of 1.75 after three rounds of spending, indicating that the initial inflow of $10,000 creates total spending and economic benefits of $17,500 ($10,000 X 1.75).

Once the multiplier is known for a given company, community or industry it can be used to estimate the economic impact of future changes, both positive and negative. Let's say the manufacturer in our example expands its operation and increases sales by $1,000,000 annually. The total economic benefit of the expansion is calculated by multiplying the $1,000,000 in sales by the multiplier of 1.75, resulting in a $1,750,000 economic benefit. Likewise, a reduction in sales of $1,000,000 will have a negative economic impact of $1,750,000.

Increasing the multiplier also increases the economic benefit and vice versa. Using the preceding example, if the local chamber of commerce implements a very effective buy local campaign and the average $2,500 spent locally on goods and services goes up to $4,000, the multiplier increases to 1.9 ($10,000 + $5,000 + $4,000/ $10,000 = 1.9. The economic benefit from the $1,000,000 sales increase improves from $1,750,000 to $1,900,000, an increase of $150,000. If over time the amount of money spent locally deceases to the original $2,500, the multiplier will revert back to 1.75 and the economic benefit will decrease by $150,000.

Note: The preceding example calculates the multiplier after three rounds of spending. Additional rounds of spending further impact the final value of the multiplier.

When announcing new projects, economists and economic developers love multipliers. It allows them to take a project's estimated value and multiply it into something bigger. Who wouldn't love turning a $100,000 project into an $180,000 project just by doing some simple multiplication? But of course, when a plant closes and multipliers increase losses, they are hardly ever mentioned.

It is important not to confuse money flow and the multiplier effect. A change in money flow is the difference between money flowing into and out of the local economy and determines the amount of money available for spending (see Chapter 2). The multiplier effect is the total economic impact a community can expect from a change in the local economy.

Part Two

Magnetic Community Strategies

When talking to colleagues and clients about Magnetic Communities, many of them question why so much of the discussion revolves around money: money flow, new money, money trail, etc. As a result, I've looked for other approaches to describe Magnetic Communities, but consider this:

- Do communities recruit new industries because they like to see people work or because they want to see residents with good jobs and money to spend?

- Do communities promote workforce training because they like smarter workers or because they want to attract higher paying jobs and residents with money to spend?

- Do communities develop tourism programs because they like to meet new people or because they want to attract visitors with money to spend?

- Do communities recruit retirees and develop retirement communities because they like old people or because they want to attract retirees who spend their savings and government benefits locally?

In reality, community wealth and personal well-being (prosperity) can be about health and happiness or about having enough money to afford healthcare and the ability to purchase a better quality of life? Money is not always the answer, but rather a measure of success. If a community's vision for the future includes prosperity, attracting and retaining money is almost always going to be part of the discussion and strategic plan for getting there.

Implementing Magnetic Community strategies that attract and retain money is not difficult. The traditional economic development strategies of industrial recruitment, tourism, retiree attraction, entrepreneurship, workforce development, etc. do not change; neither do the strategies for regional cooperation and competitiveness, but rather, they are enhanced by staying focused on money flow and not exclusively on the number of jobs and capital investment.

Residents, businesses and local governments can implement many Magnetic Community strategies without hiring additional staff. Economic developers should not fear the involvement of residents; there are many actions residents can take independent of the current economic development program to help attract and retain money. The role of the economic developer does not have to change, but assisting and coordinating these grass root efforts potentially strengthens the current economic development effort and brings additional resources to the table.

The Magnetic Community model of economic development promotes strategies that complement each other. For example, if a community can use more overnight accommodations to enhance their tourism program, why not encourage a local entrepreneur or retiree to start a bed and breakfast? The community will have a new locally owned business, a stronger tourism program and an enhanced tax base. Taking this illustration one step further, if the community can recruit a retiree from another community to relocate and start a bed and breakfast, the community will not only benefit from the relocating retiree's investment and ongoing revenue from the B&B, but also from the retiree's Social Security payments and other sources of retirement income.

In the past, economic development decisions were driven by proximity to markets, access to transportation, affordable labor, etc. Today, many business owners, entrepreneurs and employees are more interested in quality of life and sense of community than traditional location criteria. Amenities such as open space, multiuse trails and recreation are at the top of their priority list. In many instances, jobs follow people, in that people select a place they want to live and raise a family and then look for work, work remotely or start a business. Many entrepreneurs look for an ideal community before starting a business, especially those individuals who are able to live and work anywhere there is a connection to the Internet. More and more working age individuals rate the importance of community higher than a job.

Strategic Planning

Not all Magnetic Community strategies are going to work for every community. That is why communities must have a strategic plan that outlines their vision for the future. The plan helps community leaders and economic developers prioritize how best to invest their limited time and financial resources. Knowing how much new money manufacturing, tourism, retirees, etc. attract, allows economic developers determine how much emphasis to place on each industry segment. A community's strategic plan provides a comprehensive overview of the local economy and sets policy priorities for community and economic development activities. It also identifies potential strategies, programs and projects to improve the local economy. The plan identifies local workforce skills necessary to support both existing and target industries. By aligning training programs with economic development goals, communities insure that local workers are qualified to fill both existing and future jobs.

Many times the most difficult part of the strategic planning process is creating a shared vision for the community. What makes it difficult is that visioning must come first and sets the stage for the overall strategic plan. For example, the community's history buffs may have one vision while the economic developers have another, and never the twain shall meet. The situation may seem impossible, but do not give up or skip over this step. The community needs a vision before proceeding.

The Empty House

The realtor said, "It has potential."

My friend said, "Let's move on."

And I said, "Wait a minute. This may be a rundown duplex but with a little work, it can be a beautiful in-town estate."

By this time, my friend was in the car and the realtor was out on the front porch smoking a cigarette. Obviously, what I had was a personal vision, not a shared vision!

It is true; a beautiful old home chopped up into a duplex challenges the imagination of most home buyers. To some, tall ceilings, peeling paint, blocked off windows, bricked-up fire places and years of inattention create a vision of dark drafty rooms with no charm and lots of work. To others, it is an opportunity to recreate a place of beauty.

To make a long story short, I spent two years and lots of the bank's money turning 806 Myrtle Street into my vision of an in-town estate. When the dark drafty living room was completed, with its restored fireplace and French doors opening to the sunroom, everyone was able to see my vision.

By changing the name of this story to *The Empty Town*, there are several obvious parallels. The town council says, "We have potential."

Visitors, tourists and potential homebuyers say, "Let's move on!"

But I say, "Wait a minute. This town may have seen better days, but with a vision for what is possible, it can become a thriving prosperous community."

Again, to some, empty storefronts, peeling paint, over grown lots and years of inattention create a vision of a town past its prime and in need of lots of work. To others, it is an opportunity to recreate a community with historic charm and character.

If the starting point for revitalization was simply some remodeling and marketing, many more towns would be on their way to a prosperous future. But the hardest part must come first – creating a shared vision of what the revitalized town will look like. It takes leadership, public input and participation from a broad segment of the community.

Just like the living room, with its fireplace as the focal point and its French doors open to the outside, communities must also create shared visions with focal points and open themselves to the outside world. Communities around the U.S. have created visions that focus on a way of life, natural beauty, history, culture, commercial opportunities, etc. Whatever the vision, it must be shared by the community as a whole.

A Magnetic Community's strategic plan can be a simple outline (see below) or an in-depth description of what must be accomplished to move the community from where it is today to its vision of the future. By implementing strategies to attract and retain money, Magnetic Communities generate a positive cash flow and prosper.

Magnetic Community Strategic Plan

Vision (Community's vision)

I.   Goal – Prosperity (financial success and happiness)

II. Objective – Create a positive cash flow (increase the amount of money in circulation locally)

III. Strategies

    A. Attract money

    B. Retain money

One of the most productive Magnetic Community strategic planning exercises I've conducted is to ask planning participants to identify ways money flows out of the local economy. I also ask participants to list ways money is retained and circulated. This exercise keeps the primary focus on retaining money rather than on attracting money. If the planning group is made up of working residents, retirees, business owners and members of local government, the list will include a wide range of outflows and solutions.

CHAPTER 5

Community Strategies

Economic and community development efforts are part of almost every community's strategy for creating prosperity. To this end, communities endeavor to create new jobs, attract new investments, and improve the area's overall quality of life by implementing a variety of strategies. Critical to the understanding of how local development efforts impact a community's prosperity is an understanding of how individual projects impact the flow of money as it enters, circulates within, and exits the community. This basic concept, although fairly easy to understand, is seldom considered when developing strategic plans or when evaluating projects. By keeping money flow considerations in mind, community leaders and others interested in economic development are able to insure that development strategies actually pay dividends.

Community Development

Community development efforts usually support economic development strategies aimed at recruiting, expanding, retaining and starting businesses. In their own right, community development programs are instrumental in attracting and retaining money: (1) Place-based development strategies seek to leverage distinctive local assets that strengthen economic competitiveness, create jobs and build wealth while preserving what makes the place unique; (2) Economic gardening strategies take an entrepreneurial approach to creating prosperity by focusing on strategic growth challenges such as developing new markets and refining existing business models. These grow-from-within strategies help existing companies expand; (3) Community supported agriculture is a locally based economic development model for agriculture and food distribution. CSA's consist of grower and consumer networks who pledge to share the investment risks and benefits of production by receiving shares of the harvest; (4) Asset-based Community Development is an economic development strategy that seeks to uncover and use existing community strengths as a means for sustainable development and (5) Main Street investment projects encourage residents to invest in Main Street businesses rather than in Wall Street companies. Residents investing in Main Street projects circulate money in the local economy, while investments in Wall Street represent outflows.

Some small communities or sections of larger communities face retail challenges above and beyond the typical empty storefront. In these situations, it may be time to ease the rules. Relaxing zoning restrictions can attract: tiny stores, pop-up stores, artist shanties, shared space, temporary space, etc. Creativity is the key.

Activities and programs that improve the local community entice companies and people from outside the community to invest locally. For example, a resident from a neighboring town may decide to invest in a local business or a second home. When the nonresident pays property taxes on the business or second home, money is attracted to the local economy. Also, when a business headquartered in a neighboring state or community decides to establish a branch plant locally, the property tax bill is sent to the headquarters for payment, generating an inflow of money for the community. Additionally, if the branch plant employs residents, they will be paid from outside sources and their paychecks will represent new money for the community.

Many community development activities are the responsibility of local governments and include such things as: beautification, safety, recreation, parks, education, open space, redevelopment, planning, etc. A great community development program makes it easier to attract quality businesses, skilled workers, entrepreneurs, professionals, retirees, young people, home-based businesses, telecommuters, etc. By getting creative and working with the private sector, local governments can facilitate: the construction of infill housing, the donation of buildings, etc. For example, in one community I know of the city donated a historic city building to a local nonprofit that renovated it into a regional performance venue. This signature project was not a tremendous financial success but the publicity jumpstarted both the community and its economic development program.

With a "can do" attitude and some national publicity, interest in the community surged.

A strong community development effort that produces great schools, cultural and recreational opportunities, a clean safe environment, a variety of shopping and eating venues, social services and excellent medical care, help retain current residents and attract new ones. When local businesses hire employees, they can live anywhere they choose. A vibrant community with a wide range of available housing motivates local workers to live in the community, keeping their paychecks and spending local. Many economic developers think that recruiting highly paid skilled workers is going to be the next challenge for communities. Aggressive community development efforts help communities create an excellent quality of life, which can be used to recruit new residents and keep existing residents living locally.

During a brainstorming session to improve community development programs, someone asked the question "Who is our customer?" After a two-hour discussion, the group decided that their number one customer is the stay-at-home mom, or the individual, who does the shopping, entertains the kids, takes them to school and makes sure they are healthy and safe. From that point on, providing the things "mama wants" was the informal focus of the local community development program. Knowing your customer is an important first step in creating a community development program and strategy that meets the needs of the community.

Many communities within commuting distance of good paying jobs have prospered by creating bedroom communities with environments conducive to the needs of current and potential residents. At the same time, many communities with good paying jobs have been denied the prosperity they seek simply because they do not have the infrastructure and quality of life necessary to attract and retain residents. As a result, many traditional employment centers and established residential areas have suffered from an outflow of residents and money to communities with a better quality of life. The outflow of residents and money is not confined to people and paychecks. When current residents leave, or potential residents choose not to relocate, a lot of negative forces are put into motion. Stores lose customers, banks lose depositors, volunteer groups lose members, churches lose parishioners and offerings, communities lose population-based social support funding, and so forth.

Proponents of Magnetic Communities do not consider bedroom communities a sign of weakness but rather a sign of strength. In the past, communities considered their ability to attract businesses and jobs as the primary measure of success. Today, when jobs and businesses are not necessarily tied to a location, communities are better off if they measure success by their ability to attract people rather than companies and jobs. Bedroom communities attract wages without the related truck traffic, noise and congestion.

A community with a great quality of life makes it easier to recruit and retain quality businesses, skilled workers, professionals, entrepreneurs, retirees, young people, telecommuters, creative workers, engineering consultants, regional sales representatives, etc. Insuring that quality of life factors meet and exceed expectations is a Magnetic

Community strategy that applies universally to recruiting businesses, residents, tourists and retirees.

Economic Development

Conventional thinking purports that economic development is driven by private businesses relocating, expanding and starting up. These businesses may be involved in manufacturing, distribution, agriculture, transportation, research and development, business services, or other activities. Conventional thinking goes on to claim that the investments businesses make in a community give rise to a range of commercial activities and services, when in truth it is the money people make and the potential spending it creates that gives rise to commercial activities and services. Finally, it is not business growth that drives residential development; it's population growth, which in turn gives rise to further commercial activity.

Broadly defined, economic development is the sustained and concerted action of policy makers and communities to advance the economic health of a specific area or jurisdiction. The economic development process seeks to: attract private investment, expand the tax base, create and retain jobs, promote and sustain economic growth, increase personal income, raise the standard of living and create wealth. It is important to note that in most cases economic development efforts benefit and accrue to specific local jurisdictions such as towns, cities, counties, regions and states where assets are located, people work and live, and transactions take place. This also explains why economic development is a competitive process and why towns, cities, counties, regions and states fund individual economic development programs to promote and advance local interests.

To achieve economic development goals, Magnetic Communities seek to create a positive cash flow, or a net gain of money flowing into the community. Let's say a community has $5 million in circulation at any given time, $2.5 million is spent locally and stays in circulation, while the other $2.5 million exits the local economy for things like utility bills, house payments, insurance, etc. During the same time period, the community generates an inflow of $3 million from the outside sale of goods and services, and from other sources of new money. The result is a positive cash flow of $.5 million. The increase in money circulating locally ($.5 million) represents economic development.

After years of working in the field of economic and community development, I have to admit there is no universal definition of economic development. In reality, any action or transaction by a resident, business or local government to increase the inflow of money, stimulate its circulation or decrease its outflow is economic development.

On a clear sunny day in March, the mayor proudly announces the location of a new business in the local industrial park. Everyone in town is excited about the project's potential economic impact. At the groundbreaking a few months later, the local economic developer declares, "This investment in our community will create 250 good paying jobs and will increase both commercial activity and residential growth". Two years later, when the plant is up and running and there are no new stores and little new residential construction, everyone is wondering what went wrong. Even though the town may have every right to expect economic growth, private investment alone is not enough to insure increased commercial activity and residential growth. The final outcome depends on where the plant sources its raw materials, supplies and services, and where workers live and spend their paychecks.

Evidenced by the fact that economic development job descriptions, job postings and basic professional development courses remain focused on attracting manufacturing plants and jobs, many of today's economic development strategies and programs are based on business recruitment practices that have not changed in the past 50 years. As a result, money and resources are wasted on efforts that do little to create and improve prosperity. In addition, these strategies and programs are almost entirely focused on attracting money, with little regard for retaining money already in circulation. From a Magnetic Community perspective, economic development efforts seek to advance local prosperity by both attracting and retaining money. The overall objective is to create a positive cash flow, or a net gain of money flowing into the local economy. This is accomplished by increasing the amount of money flowing into the community and by decreasing the amount of money flowing out, or both.

Economic development success at any cost seems to be the strategy of some communities. I started watching the development of a nearby industrial park and talking to the county developer soon after the county purchased the land. The site was near the county line adjacent to a prosperous urban county. The county developer told me that they had lost several recent projects because the county's work force was largely unskilled. By siting the new industrial park adjacent to the urban county, they were able to create a much better labor profile for the park. The county's regional partnership supported the project because the new park was centrally located in the region. After adding a shell building, the county eventually recruited an industry.

When all was said and done, the county created jobs and increased the tax base; but incentives awarded to the new industry almost entirely absorbed the new tax revenues. In addition, locally sourced materials, parts, supplies, and services almost exclusively came from the nearby urban counties. Approximately, eighty percent of the plant's workforce commuted into the county each morning and back home each evening where they spent most of their earnings.
When discussing the project with the economic developer and local leaders, no one wanted to admit that the industrial park's location was a bad idea. In fact, when discussing existing economic development projects, it is very difficult for an elected official, public sector manager, or economic developer to admit a mistake. They are usually paid entirely, or in part, with public funds and do not want to admit short comings to the electorate who directly or indirectly control their employment and pay.

Many economic developers believe that economic development does not include selling things to each other. I disagree. Selling things to each other keeps money circulating in the local economy. It is true that tourists having lunch at a local diner attracts money to the local economy and that residents having the same lunch does not attract new money, but rather circulates money. Because new money and existing money create the same economic benefit when being spent, Magnetic Communities consider both transactions economic development. They also consider convincing a resident to have lunch locally rather than driving to a neighboring town as economic development.

Which of the following is economic development?

- Fresh vegetables purchased from a local farmer by a resident? (Y – Money is retained and circulated in the local economy)

- A paycheck earned at a local manufacturing plant by an employee living in a neighboring community? (N – Money flows out of the local economy when the employee drives home and spends the paycheck.)

- A paycheck earned by a resident at a manufacturing plant in a neighboring county? (Y – Money is attracted and flows into the local economy when the employee drives home and spends the paycheck locally.)

- A paycheck earned by a resident at a local manufacturing plant? (Y – Money is retained and circulates in the local economy)

- A local machine shop makes and sells parts to a local manufacturer? (Y – Money is retained and circulates in the local economy)

- A retired resident receives a Social Security Check from the Federal government? (Y – Money is attracted and flows into the local economy from the Federal Government)

- A tourist pays the admission fee to a local attraction owned and operated by the state? (N – If this is the tourist's only purchase, the admission fee flows back to the state capital.)

Magnetic Community principles are woven into, but do not change, traditional economic development strategies such as: business recruitment, expansion, retention, entrepreneurship, tourism, workforce development, regional cooperation, etc. As the global economic development landscape evolves, businesses will continue to adapt their business strategies and site selection criteria to maximize profit and minimize risk. These moves will undoubtedly produce situations where communities prepared with a traditional economic development strategy, such as a certified industrial site and/or a speculative building, will be rewarded.

CHAPTER 6

Business Strategies

Businesses are traditionally grouped into three categories: primary industries, manufacturing industries and service industries. Because of their importance and contribution to the prosperity of Magnetic Communities, two service industry sub groups: creative industries and nonprofits are highlighted separately.

Primary industries make direct use of natural resources and include activities like agriculture, forestry, fishing, mining and the extraction of oil and gas. New money is generated when local products such as corn, lumber, seafood, gravel and petroleum are sold outside the community. Money is retained when primary industries sell products locally and when they purchase local materials, supplies, services and labor to conduct business activities.

Manufacturing continues to be an important economic development strategy. Recruiting, expanding, retaining and starting manufacturing industries continue to be the foundation of many economic development programs. When a local manufacturing plant makes a product and sells it in the global marketplace, new money flows back to the community. Money is retained when manufacturing industries sell products locally, employ residents and purchase local materials, supplies and services.

In general, service industries include all businesses that are not classified as primary or manufacturing. Traditionally, service industries had two disadvantages over manufacturing industries. First, they paid lower wages, and second they often provided services to local businesses and residents, which circulated money but did not attract new money to the community. In today's technology-based economy, many service sector jobs pay wages equal to or greater than manufacturing jobs. Similar to manufacturing, many service sector businesses sell their services outside the local economy and attract new money to the community. As most local economies become more service-oriented, communities need to elevate their thinking about service companies and work to maximize their economic impact. Money is retained when service industries sell services locally, employ residents and purchase local materials, supplies and services.

Technically, creative industries are included in the service sector, but because this segment of the economy is growing and has so much potential to create prosperity, it is viewed separately. The creative industry sector includes activities by artists, fashion designers, filmmakers, musicians, architects, inventors, authors, software developers, research and development workers, engineering consultants and others. When evaluating the economic benefits of creative industries, it is helpful to follow the money trail for each business or category of business. For example, local artists may sell paintings to tourists out of their studio, on the Internet and on consignment to galleries outside the community. The artists may also be part of a larger art community that brings events and recognition to the community. Following the money trail may reveal multiple outside money streams, along with a support role for tourism and the local art scene.

Most people are amazed when they find out how many local and regional nonprofits operate in their community. These businesses usually exist for a specific purpose and generate income from a wide variety of grants, fund raising and fees for service. Grants from outside agencies, foundations and governments almost always represent new money for the local economy. Nonprofits are businesses, and like other businesses, they rent office space, purchase supplies, develop websites, pay utilities, employ auditors, establish banking relationships, etc. Local nonprofit employees pay rent, purchase homes, shop, dine out, buy cars, etc., all of which benefit the local economy.

Magnetic Community business strategies differ from traditional economic development strategies in that success is measured in terms of money flow rather than capital investment and jobs. Capital investment and jobs are still important, but only to the extent that they contribute to the attraction and retention of money.

Attract Money Strategies

Recruit, Expand, Start and Retain Businesses that Sell Products and Provide Services Outside the Local Economy

When local businesses make products and provide services sold outside the community, money is attracted to the local economy. By recruiting, expanding, starting and retaining these businesses, communities are able to increase and maintain the amount of money in circulation and available locally for spending. By exporting goods and services, not necessarily outside the country, communities create trade surpluses and positive flows of money into the local economy.

Recruiting businesses to a community is usually not a problem when the relocating company is moving a long distance. In contrast, recruiting businesses from neighboring towns can do more harm than good, especially going forward when the success of recruiting future companies requires regional cooperation. Magnetic Communities work to attract and retain as much money as possible, but not to the detriment of local and regional alliances.

With that in mind, many small companies are started in communities where the founding entrepreneur lives. As the company grows and establishes branch locations, the original store's location may no longer be optimal for long-term growth. By staying in touch with the local stores and by making occasional contact with the regional office, communities may be able to take advantage of relocation opportunities that were going to take place anyway. Communities may also find recruitment and expansion opportunities by taking note of out-of-town company vehicles making service calls locally.

These companies are in some cases driving long distances to service customers. A little research may uncover an opportunity to establish a local branch location. Over the years, I have successfully worked with pest control companies, electricians, and HVAC companies, all spotted from my desk at the Chamber of Commerce.

When communities successfully recruit new businesses from outside the local economy, ones that use local contractors, suppliers and workers to build the new plant, workers are paid with money generated outside the local economy. Even if branch businesses lease existing space and pay local contractors and suppliers to up-fit buildings, new money is attracted to the community. Once the businesses are in operation and the companies' products and services are sold outside the local economy, new money continues to be attracted to the community.

Illustration 8

Locally Owned Businesses Sell Goods and Services to Customers outside the Local Economy

Magnetic Communities recognize that locally owned businesses selling products and services outside the community generate more income for the community than branch businesses.

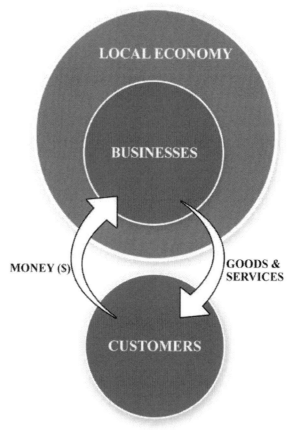

When locally owned businesses sell goods and services to customers outside the local economy, new money flows into the community and to locally owned businesses.

Illustration 9

Local Businesses, Not Locally Owned, Sell Goods and Services to Customers outside the Local Economy

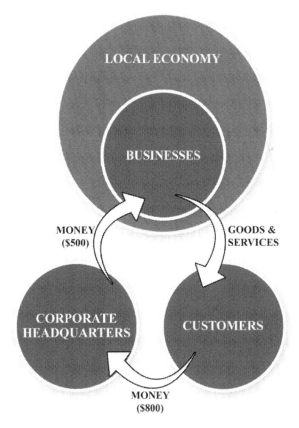

When local branch businesses sell goods and services to customers outside the local economy, payments pass through the corporate office of the branch businesses on its way back to the community. Because branch businesses are not locally owned, profits are retained by the corporate office and do not benefit the local economy. If the corporate office keeps $300 of the $800 as profit, the local branch businesses receive $500 rather than the full $800, as in the case of locally owned businesses.

Starting new businesses that attract outside money is an effective Magnetic Community strategy. This is not to discount larger established firms that contribute to the local economy, but entrepreneurship and small business development can be an even more effective job creator. Start-ups drive both economic growth and contribute to the creation of additional start-ups. By facilitating and incentivizing entrepreneurship, communities create new jobs, stimulate creativity, increase spending and most importantly, create new sources of money for the local economy.

Many entrepreneurial endeavors start out and remain home-based businesses, but just because they are home-based does not mean they are small or marginally profitable. Technology-based businesses that provide consulting, programming and other technical services can grow quickly, generously rewarding owners, investors, employees and the local economy. I recently met the owner of a local bakery whose day job was computer support. This entrepreneur was not only helping to retain money by providing technical services to local businesses, but also attracting new money by providing services to regional clients, while his wife ran the bakery business. To make this an even better story, the couple purchased and renovated the downtown building they were leasing, moved upstairs and operated the bakery down stairs.

Entrepreneurs are a special breed of business owners. Once they have a business up and running, they are just as likely to start another business, as they are to expand an existing one. I've seen a sandwich shop owner start a bakery because quality bread was hard to find. Later, the same entrepreneur started a butcher shop and subsequently another restaurant. Helping entrepreneurs does not produce the big ground breaking ceremony but it does stimulate investment and job creation.

Many startups are small and funded at levels that make it possible for residents and other small businesses to invest. For example, in a small town without a pizza restaurant or dry cleaners, several local entrepreneurs decided to start a shopping/delivery service. Initially, they hired a recent high school graduate to do the driving, take orders and pickup/deliver pizzas. Later the entrepreneurs started the dry cleaning pickup and delivery service, and as business grew they expanded into other pickup and delivery services. Much of the start-up funding, which was minimal, was raised locally. Because each business and community is different, the best approach for moving forward on a new business idea is creativity. Potential entrepreneurs can approach community banks, local investors and other small business owners for funding and technical assistance. Local revolving loan funds, crowd funding, venture capital, small business incubators, cooperatives and most of all, networking opportunities, are all potential resource opportunities for entrepreneurs.

Expand, Retain and Start Locally Owned and Operated Businesses

Locally owned and operated businesses not only have the potential to attract new money from the sale of products and services outside the local economy, but they also retain profits earned by the businesses. Illustration 8 (page 72) shows the money flow of locally owned and operated businesses selling products to customers outside the local economy. Illustration

9 (page 73) shows the same transaction but with outside ownership of the businesses.

Locally owned and operated businesses are more likely to use local services such as engineering, legal, banking, accounting, insurance, etc. Many locally owned businesses are also headquartered locally, which is likely to include higher paid functions associated with management, payroll, marketing, research and sales. Locally operated and headquartered businesses attract meetings, conferences and marketing calls from vendors who stay in hotels, eat at restaurants, purchase gas, etc. With roots in the community, locally owned and operated businesses are not as sensitive to cost increases and are more likely to sponsor events, reinvest locally, hire local workers, volunteer, mentor, donate to local charities, serve on boards and contribute to local charities. Locally owned businesses also add to the character, culture and uniqueness of a community.

Magnetic Communities look at the benefits of locally owned and operated businesses and realize that starting, expanding and retaining locally owned businesses have real potential for creating prosperity. An important subset of locally owned and operated businesses includes family owned businesses. These firms have all the positive attributes of locally owned and operated businesses and in many cases grow as fast as or faster than nonfamily owned firms.

Add Value to Local Products and Services Sold Outside the Local Economy

Increasing the value of products and services sold outside the community increases the amount of money flowing back into the local economy. For example, many farmers sell their harvests in bulk on commodity markets. Even though this generates a flow of money into the community, the money flow can be increased by adding value to the harvest. For example, the simple act of branding a product increases recognition and opens up opportunities to differentiate products from competitors. Other examples of adding value include turning cucumbers into pickles, onions into relish, strawberries into jam, etc. Many farmers have considered this strategy, but faced obstacles such as funding, regulations and/or a lack of knowledge and expertise.

From a global manufacturing perspective, I remember a local technology based company in the business of making high value products always reporting steady production and job growth. On a regular visit to the plant, I found out that the production of high value products made with skilled labor were being moved to Ireland while low value products made with unskilled labor were being moved to the local plant. The move was precipitated by a lack of locally available skilled labor. Adding value is a good strategy for attracting outside revenue but keeping a workforce's skill level current can also be a challenge and represents one more reason why the total number of jobs is not a good measure of economic development success.

Expand Markets Beyond the Local Economy

Helping local businesses and nonprofits expand sales and fundraising beyond the local economy attracts new money to the community. Many small businesses and nonprofits look to their immediate community for customers and donors. Residents of neighboring towns also want to support disadvantaged citizens, medical research, first responders, animal shelters, etc. There is no reason to limit sales and fundraising to a particular community. Look to the Internet and neighboring towns for sales and funding. Not only will your business or charity have more money to spend but your community will also benefit. It is important to support the charities and nonprofits of your choice, but it is also important to remember that a check written to the local Red Cross circulates money and helps people locally, whereas a check written to the national Red Cross is an outflow for the community.

One of my favorite examples of expanding sales beyond the local economy comes from a small southern town with a local country restaurant. The business was barely making ends meet when the owner put a billboard on the interstate that read something to the effect, "World's Worst Apple Pie 5 miles." In no time, tourists, casual travelers, truckers and sales representatives traveling the interstate were a major source of new money for the restaurant and the community. By the way, the apple pie was great.

Local electricians, house painters, computer repair technicians, etc. who have traditionally restricted their business to local clients all have the potential to expand beyond the local economy. Some business owners may not want to expand but others will welcome the support and resources a community can identify and provide. For example, assisting a local machine shop acquire the certification necessary to supply parts to the aerospace industry expands the local company's market, potentially attracts new money and creates an additional support service that can be marketed to other aerospace companies.

Retain Money Strategies

Even though new money is not attracted to a community when local businesses sell goods and services to local customers, money is retained in the local economy. Money that is retained: continues to circulate, remains available for future spending and is subject to economic multipliers (See Chapter 4).

Illustration 10

Locally Owned Businesses Sell Goods and Services to Local Customers

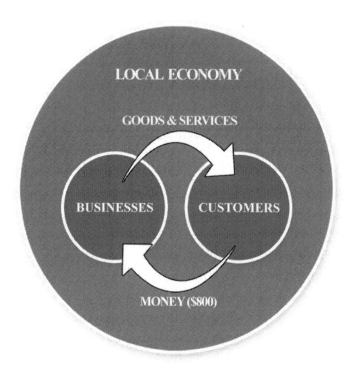

When locally owned businesses sell $800 in goods and services to local customers, $800 flows directly from customers to businesses, retaining and circulating money in the local economy, including profits to local owners.

Illustration 11

Local Businesses, Not Locally Owned, Sell Goods and Services to Local Customers

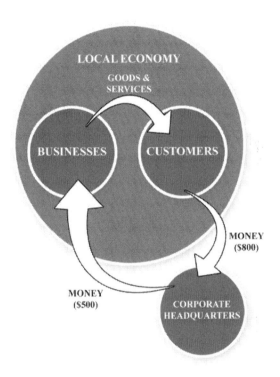

When local branch businesses sell $800 in goods and services to local customers, $800 flows out of the local economy and through the corporate headquarters, before making its way back to the local economy. If the corporate owners retain $300 in expenses and profits, the local benefit is a minus $300.

Illustration 12

Local businesses purchase goods and services from local suppliers

When local businesses purchase goods and services from local suppliers, money circulates in the local economy and is retained.

Identify Local Sources for Raw Materials, Supplies and Services

When local businesses purchase local materials, supplies and services, money circulates in the community. Because new money is both scarce and valuable, Magnetic Communities work with local businesses to keep money in circulation as long as possible. Local businesses must not overlook the potential spending of institutional buyers such as hospitals, colleges, school districts and local governments. Regional and national sales representatives understand their value and may be selling products, supplies and services to local institutions right under the noses of local companies. Identifying local suppliers or local businesses capable of providing the required goods and services represents an opportunity to improve the community's cash flow equation. This may also be an opportunity for a local entrepreneur to start a business. Of course, local businesses are free to source goods and services from any number of places, and I'm not suggesting that local businesses be strong-armed or coerced into purchasing goods and services locally, but if an opportunity exists, Magnetic Communities will identify and promote ways to strengthen local connections and linkages.

Making businesses aware of locally available materials, products and services, along with the economic benefits of buying locally, is an amazingly easy and cost effective way to retain money. As long as local businesses remain competitive and do not have to go out of their way to identify and purchase local materials, supplies and services, they are usually willing to do the right thing and make purchases locally.

Illustration 13

Local businesses purchase goods and services from suppliers outside the local economy

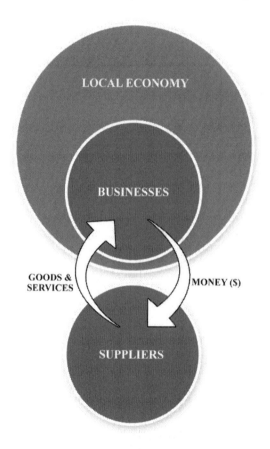

When local businesses purchase goods and services from outside suppliers, money flows out of the local economy.

Recruit, Expand, Retain and Start Businesses to Fill Gaps in Locally Available Materials, Supplies and Services

When local businesses purchase local materials, supplies and services, money is retained and circulates in the community. If gaps exist, businesses are forced to make outside purchases, creating money outflows. When Magnetic Communities identify gaps, they work to stem the outflow by recruiting and starting businesses to fill the gaps. The first option is to approach the current supplier and see if they are willing to establish a local branch plant. An alternative to recruiting or starting a business is to find a local business in a similar field and evaluate the feasibility and their willingness to expand or add a product line. It is also important to make sure that suppliers of local goods and services remain successful and in business. Losing a supplier can be devastating, especially if the supplier's customers are also negatively impacted. The last thing a community wants to see is both a supplier and local business close.

Anytime a community identifies goods, services, raw materials, etc. being imported into the local economy, a Magnetic Community's response is to find ways of replacing these imports with local products. By doing so, communities are able to stop or reduce money outflows and increase the amount of money available for spending locally. From time to time, a successful import replacement effort results in an opportunity to export goods and services. For example, if a community lacks a caterer for local civic events and must import the service from outside the community, there may be an opportunity for a local restaurant or resident to fill the gap.

By replacing the imported service with a local service, money stays in the local economy. If the new catering business becomes successful and recognized for its quality and service, opportunities may open up to provide catering services outside the local economy, creating an inflow of money. The community will have executed a Magnetic Community hat trick by eliminating an outflow, starting a business and creating an inflow. Even though the term *trade balance* is most often used to describe goods and services moving between countries, it also applies to communities. The preceding example illustrates how a small community improved its trade balance by growing from within. Continuing success in import replacement efforts improves a community's cash flow and ability to prosper. Import replacement and localization efforts are not an attempt at self-sufficiency or isolation, but are made in the spirit of self-determination.

Entrepreneurship is one of the most effective economic development strategies available to communities. A successful local startup may not only provide a missing product or service, but also keeps wages, profits and ownership close to home.

When I was teaching entrepreneurial classes, one of the first questions I regularly received was, "What kind of a business should I start?" Knowing what local products and services are missing, answers the question for entrepreneurs and if successful, keeps money circulating locally.

Identify and Hire Qualified Local Workers

Filling local job openings with residents or nonresidents who are willing to relocate is not always an easy proposition, but if successful, pays substantial dividends. Convincing a nonresident to relocate is comparable to hiring a resident. Illustrations 14 and 15, pages 88 and 89 set up the money flow situation for both residents and in-commuting nonresidents.

Assisting local businesses identify and hire qualified local workers retains money in the local economy. Even though employees can live where they choose, Magnetic Communities do everything possible to help workers live locally. Giving hiring preferences to residents and workers willing to relocate strengthens the relationship between businesses, workers, and the community. Communities that assist in the relocation process and provide incentives to live locally are implementing strategies that create prosperity. Also, by developing training programs, internships and online job registries, communities create an environment that promotes local employment and job growth. Aggressively marketing the community and convincing transferees to live locally is essential to keeping paychecks working in the local

Illustration 14

Local Businesses Employ Residents

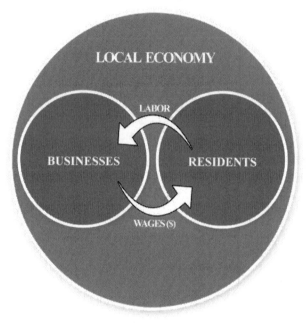

When local businesses employ and pay resident-labor, money is retained and circulates in the local economy.

Illustration 15

Local Businesses Employ Nonresidents

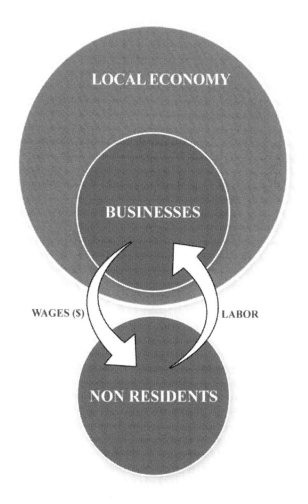

When local businesses employ and pay nonresidents, money flows out of the local economy and is no longer available to provide economic benefits. Working with local businesses to identify qualified resident-employees and to convince prospective nonresident employees to relocate are both Magnetic Community strategies that positively impact a community's cash flow.

economy. Living locally benefits both workers by shortening their commute and businesses by strengthening their image as good corporate citizens.

If business incentives are part of the discussion in a business relocation or expansion decision, it is important to bring up local hiring. Most companies want to be good corporate citizens and will agree to work with the community to hire locally qualified workers.

The ability to easily commute, telecommute or work from home provides a real challenge for communities located near resorts and areas of natural beauty such as beaches, lakes and mountains. I was reminded of this when attending a business meeting where a new plant manager was asked by a very proud chamber president why the company chose their community. The answer was short, "...the beach" and the silence was excruciating. Also, rural communities with good jobs may have a hard time convincing workers to live in the community when the school system and other quality of life factors are not as good as those in neighboring urban communities.

Convert In-Commuters to Residents

Converting local workers living outside the community into residents helps retain money. Not only are in-commuters taking jobs from residents, they are taking money out of the local economy. They may buy gas and lunch from time to time but the bulk of their spending is most likely taking place where they live.

If a substantial number of local workers, especially highly paid workers, choose to live outside the community, their paychecks and associated spending are going to leave with the employee on payday and provide little, if any benefit to the local economy. With direct deposit, paychecks probably never even enter the local economy, but rather go straight to the in-commuter's bank account. Because highly paid workers have more resources and options about where they live or where to have second homes, the outflow of money can be substantial. If local doctors, plant managers and business owners live outside the community, or live locally and leave for the beach on Friday afternoon, the local economy is not going to fully benefit from their income and potential spending.

In most cases, a worker's natural inclination is to reduce the time, distance and cost of commuting. If workers continue to commute, it is important to know why they commute and why they are not willing to move closer to work and become part of the community. There are always reasons like family, a spouse's job, etc. that no one can overcome. But, if quality of life issues related to education, housing, recreation and safety are the reasons for not moving, the community's focus needs to be on community development. A starting point is to survey local employers to determine the number of employees and the amount of pay flowing out of the local economy. A simple spreadsheet with home zip codes and take-home pay will determine the scope of the issue, but it will take a more in-depth community development analysis to determine the reasons behind the problem.

Request Transferees and New Hires to Live Locally

When local businesses interview potential employees, convincing them to live locally helps retain money and stops a potential outflow. It is usually easier to convince a transferee or new hire to live locally during the hiring process than to convince them to move later.

Communities lose a lot of economic benefit by not getting involved early on with the personnel directors of new and expanding companies. It is the community's responsibility to market the community to transferees. Once transferees make a decision not to live locally, their paychecks and spending are probably lost for quite some time. Additionally, once a top executive or other transferee makes a decision on where to live, others are likely to follow. If that decision is to live locally, great! But if the decision is to in-commute, the negative consequences can be significant.

Local businesses that understand and support Magnetic Community strategies are able to make a big difference in the growth and prosperity of the community. By giving local job applicants preference and by requesting that new hires and transferees relocate to the community, local businesses are able to keep wages working locally, improving both local prosperity and the community's business environment. When communities recognize and understand what creates prosperity, they can put many Magnetic Community and money flow strategies to work.

CHAPTER 7

Tourist Strategies

Tourists are an excellent source of new money. How much easier can it be? Individuals travel to a community at their own expense, open their wallets, make purchases and drive off. Yes, tourists actually pay their own shipping by traveling to pick up their merchandise. In addition, individuals and families travel through communities every day; the only thing a community has to do is find a reason for them to stop and make a purchase. Unless they rob a local bank on the way out of town, money is not going to leave the community.

Tourists include individuals from outside the community such as shoppers, visitors, travelers, sightseers, etc. They may be vacationing, attending an athletic event, business meeting, summer camp, or enjoying a local festival. Communities with specialized medical facilities, athletic training venues, etc. also stand to benefit from visitor spending.

Attracting tourists to a community is one thing, getting them to spend is quite another. A community with a museum, arts center, athletic stadium, or festival may attract visitors, but if there are no convenient restaurants, gift shops and places to stay, the economic benefits are going to be limited.

Spending at tourism venues, shops, restaurants and overnight accommodations attracts money to the local economy. Communities must keep in mind that tourism without spending produces no economic benefit! If the overall tourism goal is to attract new money, then increasing tourist spending must be the primary objective.

Over my career I have enjoyed living in tourist areas where I took advantage of the same amenities that attract tourists. As a resident, my spending did not attract new money, but it did circulate money I already had in my wallet and bank account. Eating in local seafood restaurants and paying to go tubing down a local river both added to the vitality of the local economy and to the revenue of local businesses. As with other Magnetic Community strategies, tourism enhances quality of life amenities and attracts businesses, residents and retirees to the community as well.

Some communities are fortunate to be located near bodies of water, mountain ranges, historic sites or other culturally significant areas. Many communities have created attractions such as amusement parks, outlet malls, golf courses, wineries, marinas or have revitalized downtowns to attract visitors and tourists. Still others may find themselves on the main thoroughfare leading to a major tourist or visitor destination, creating opportunities to provide overnight lodging, food service and other travel related goods and services. In any case, when a tourist or out of town visitor spends money; it provides the local economy with new money.

It is important to think through a community's tourism strategy to make sure new money is both attracted and retained. A local performance venue may seem like a good strategy to attract regional visitors and their money, but if after the money is invested and the facility opens, it is discovered that patrons come to evening performances when stores are closed and they leave without spending much money, the upfront investment may not be justified. I have seen this happen several times for different reasons. Primary among them is the failure of the community to insure that merchants are open before and after performances and that they carry products visitors are interested in purchasing. A second problem with this model is that money from ticket sales flows into the community and right back out when the performers are paid and leave. In addition, most performance venues have small staffs, making the amount of money retained very small compared to the effort required and the amount of money passing through the facility. The most important benefit of a performance venue may be a quality of life amenity valued by local residents.

When tourists walk into a visitor center and the attendant asks them to sign the register or guest book, the attendant is probably justifying his or her job. One of the easiest ways to document visitor activity is to have people sign a guest book.

The problem is that a guest book is a great record of restroom stops but not spending, which is really what elected officials, local businesses and other funding partners are looking to determine. A better approach is to have the attendant spend time talking with visitors about what brings them to the area, what interests them and what can the tourism representative do to help plan their stay. Counting and reporting the number of visitors is the wrong measure. Enlisting local merchants to report on spending activity is the true measure of success.

Tourism continues to be a very lucrative industry. By establishing welcome centers, hiring tourism directors and developing tourism strategies, communities look to attract tourists and money. The influx of new money is going to be directly related to the number of tourists, the quality of attractions, the length of stay, the number of spending opportunities and the overall quality of the experience. For example, a great heritage tourism site is of little economic value if there are no opportunities to spend beyond the price of admission. Remember, tourism without spending does not add or circulate money!

Attract Money Strategies

Increase Tourist Spending

More tourists almost always mean more spending and new money flowing into the local economy. Tourists have a wide range of interests and travel to communities for many reasons. Experimenting with different strategies to increase the number of tourists will most likely identify both strengths and weaknesses. By leveraging strengths and improving weaknesses, communities are able to increase tourist spending. Communities generally attract tourists, visitors, outside shoppers by marketing, advertising, branding, leveraging natural resources, etc.

Market the Community

The obvious approach to marketing is to advertise in tourism related magazines, visitor centers, billboards, websites and social media. Word of mouth marketing is probably the best and most effective way to increase the number of tourists. Marketing is even more effective when communities join together and cooperatively market a region or group of attractions.

Illustration 16

Tourists Purchase Goods and Services from Local Businesses

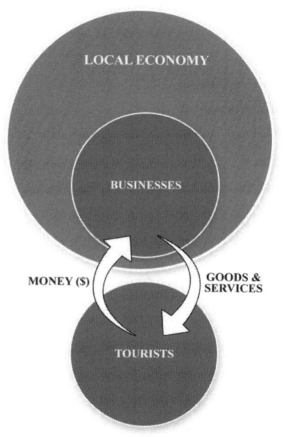

Tourists include visitors and nonresidents who are not part of the local economy. When they spend money purchasing goods and services from local businesses, new money is attracted to the local economy.

Develop and Build a Community Brand

A community with a brand, something they are known for, distinguishes one community from another and makes it easier for tourists to remember a good time. Incorporating a community's brand or promise into ongoing events is an effective strategy for promoting a community. A tagline such as the Outer Banks in North Carolina or Low Country in South Carolina also helps distinguish one area from another.

Improve the Overall Experience

People travel to enjoy themselves, to learn and to be entertained. Creating a pleasant memorable experience entices visitors to recommend a community to friends and neighbors. Because tourists expect sites to be friendly and safe, communities must insure that a tourist friendly infrastructure greets each and every visitor. A high level of hospitality, information, clean restrooms, pedestrian friendly attractions/ commercial areas, convenient/safe parking and clear signage are all things tourists and visitors look for in a tourism-friendly community. Superior tourism infrastructure attracts more tourists who stay longer, return often and spend more money.

Increase the Length of Stay

The longer a tourist is in a community the more likely they are to spend. The goal of many tourism programs is to increase the number of "heads in beds," acknowledging that tourists who spend the night are a valuable commodity.

Once a tourist shows up in a community, the goal becomes to keep them and their spending as long as possible. This is where the number of attractions and the availability of overnight accommodations become important. Most beach communities do a good job of increasing and diversifying the number and kinds of attractions. The beach may initially attract a group of tourists but if there is nothing else of interest to occupy their time, or when the weather does not cooperate, the odds of keeping tourists and their spending decreases. More things to do and see, along with more options to spend the night, increase a tourist's length of stay. Developing tourism packages with both day trips and overnight itineraries give tourists options and increases spending.

Develop Regional Alliances and Cooperation

Developing regional alliances with other communities is one way to increase the number of tourists, attractions and length of stay. For example, by creating a heritage trail that includes multiple communities and allows tourists to travel along the trail provides new money to the region and individual communities. Regional trail themes include local artisans, wineries, antique stores, music, etc.

Increase the Number and Quality of Attractions

The number, quality and variety of attractions directly impact the number of tourists who can find something that interests them. Tourists who are not satisfied with the experience or who are disappointed leave sooner and spend less.

Increasing the number of attractions builds critical mass and widens the range of appeal for seniors, adults and children. The potential list of attractions is as long as a community's ability to be creative. Examples include: shopping, kayaking, historic home tours, meetings, conventions, package tours, recreation (hunting, birding, boating, walking, hiking, biking), festivals, resorts, community theater, etc. In one community, a resident created topiaries that attracted visitors from the region and beyond. Another community commissioned a local artist to paint murals on the sides of vacant buildings, creating an outdoor art gallery.

Destination businesses are those that tourists and visitors specifically identify as places they want to visit. In other words, a destination business is an establishment that warrants a special trip. Examples include: specialty restaurants, breweries, wineries, antique stores, art galleries, flea markets, thrift stores, factory outlets, specialty gift/souvenir stores, etc.

Increase the Number of Spending Opportunities

Because tourism without spending is of little or no economic value, Magnetic Communities increase the numbers and types of tourist and visitor-related businesses. Successful communities create affordable retail spaces for small businesses by subdividing large spaces and by creating multi-tenant spaces. Subdividing large spaces also creates a cluster of shops which establishes the critical mass necessary to attract tourists. Affordable retail space encourages entrepreneurs and retirees to start locally-owned businesses that serve the tourist trade. If the tourist attraction is a historic site or natural attraction, communities must provide opportunities for tourists to spend beyond the price of admission, or the benefit will be lost. By routing traffic to and from tourist sites past shopping and eating establishments, tourists get to where they are going and merchants have an opportunity to sell products.

Increase the Value of Products and Services

Communities can increase the amount of new money attracted to the community by increasing the value and price of items for sale. Fine dining, original art and handmade jewelry may not fit all tourist destinations, but higher spending is the result of both increases in sales volume and from higher priced goods, products and services. An example from Charleston, SC is the sweet grass basket sold by locals in markets and along the highways leading into the city. These baskets have increased in quality, demand and price, making them a major contributor to the local tourist economy.

Recruit, Expand, Retain and Start Businesses that Make and/or Sell Products and Provide Services to Tourists

Again, if the goal is to attract more money to the local economy, recruiting, expanding, retaining and starting businesses that cater to tourists are all viable strategies. Starting tourism-based businesses is especially attractive to Magnetic Communities. These businesses are usually locally owned and create more local economic benefits than chain stores. Opportunities to start businesses in the tourism sector are plentiful and in many cases can be started with a minimal investment. Young people with lots of energy can start a bicycle taxi service, purchase a food truck, take tourists on kayaking adventures or become fishing guides. Retirees can leverage a hobby or special interest to occupy their time, entertain tourists and make a little extra money.

I met one retiree with a real talent for wood working. He started making wooden toys in his garage and selling them on consignment in local stores. After a while I saw that he was becoming disenchanted with the toy making business. Asked why, he told me that working by himself at home gave him very little interaction with the public and the children he wanted to make happy. When made aware of the situation, a downtown property owner found room for the toy maker in the tourist district. The retiree made wooden toys in the back of the store while greeting visitors, talking to children and selling wooden toys up front. As it turned out, everything about this arrangement was positive for the community, local tourism, the wooden toy business, and the retiree.

Not all good ideas have good outcomes. Another local retiree who wanted to start a tourist related business decided on a candle shop. He ordered inventory and waited for customers. The customers actually did show up but not in the volume necessary to cover expenses. Had the shop owner followed in the footsteps of the wooden toy maker and combined both making and selling candles in the same store, his business plan would have been much more attainable. Along the same lines, this is why many art galleries are owned and staffed by the artist, have other artists' works for sale, incorporate a frame shop, teach art/photography classes, etc. Few shop owners have the luxury of sitting behind the cash register to watch the money role in.

Recruiting outside tourism-related businesses becomes more viable when local tourism is already established. Businesses from outside the community are usually risk adverse and prefer to make investments in established tourist areas. They are looking for traffic counts, sales volume and other measures that predict success.

Assist Local Businesses Sell to Tourists

Many local businesses define their market as the surrounding community, which excludes them from the benefits of tourism. As communities, especially downtowns, evolve from traditional retail centers to tourist destinations, it is essential that merchants transition their product lines to appeal to both residents and tourists. This transition helps merchants stay in business and keeps the local business district viable. By helping local businesses tap into tourism spending, new money not only enters but circulates in the local economy.

Almost every community has had to deal with the development of a bypass and the introduction of the big box store. This phenomenon disrupts the local retail market and shifts spending for everyday goods and services to the bypass. In many small towns, this shift to the bypass is already a reality. As downtowns continue to reinvent themselves, local businesses must adapt their product mix to accommodate the change in shoppers. I have seen independent grocery stores add souvenirs, deli sandwiches, beach supplies, fishing equipment, etc. A local hardware store may add souvenirs, specialty garden items, clothing, flowers for the rental house, locally branded canned goods, etc.

If a tourist stops at a local restaurant serving meals made with locally grown and raised products, money enters and stays in the local economy. If the same tourist decides to stop at a Cracker Barrel, money enters the local economy but flows right back out when outside owners and suppliers take their share.

Retain Money Strategies

Increase the Number of Locally Produced and Grown Products Available For Sale to Tourists

When tourists spend money on locally produced and grown products, money enters the local economy and maintains its potential to benefit other residents as it circulates. For example, if two artists, one from the community and the other from out of town, sell a painting to a tourist at a local gallery. The money paid to the local artist has a greater chance of being re-spent and circulated locally. Compare this to the out of town artist who most likely takes the money and spends it back home.

Illustration 17

Local Art Gallery Sells Painting by Resident Artist

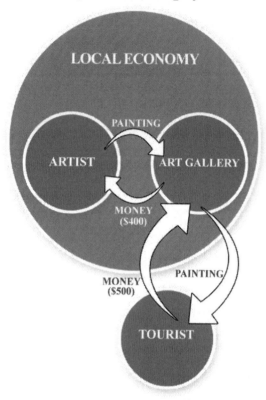

When a tourist spends $500 to purchase a resident's painting from a local art gallery, money flows into the local economy. When the art gallery pays the local artist $400 for the painting and keeps a $100 commission, the entire $500 is attracted and retained.

Illustration 18

Local Art Gallery Sells Painting by Nonresident Artist

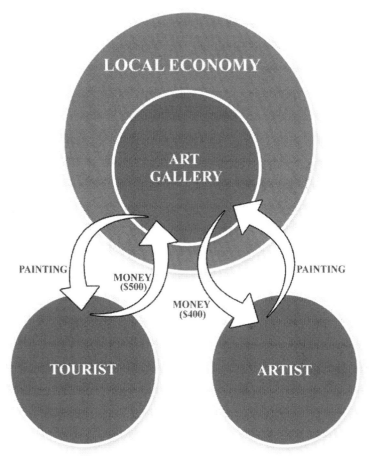

When a tourist spends $500 purchasing a nonresident's painting from a local art gallery, money flows into the local economy. When the art gallery pays the nonresident artist $400 for the painting and keeps a $100 commission, only $100 of the tourist's $500 remains in the local economy. The $400 paid to the nonresident artist flows out of the local economy. If the owner of the art gallery is interested in supporting local economic development efforts, he or she will make every effort to carry and market creations by local artists.

Increase the Number of Locally Owned and Operated Businesses Selling Products and Services to Tourists

Locally owned and operated tourism businesses have a vested interest in the local tourism market and benefit from community efforts to retain money. Rather than attempting to recruit tourism-based businesses from outside the community, local leaders should encourage resident entrepreneurs and retirees to start businesses that sell products and provide services to tourists. Locally owned and operated businesses have a proven record of hiring local workers, reinvesting profits and spending locally on products and services.

Hire Local Workers and Purchase Materials, Products, Supplies and Services Locally

Once a tourist spends money in a community, the goal is to keep it circulating as long as possible. By hiring residents, and by purchasing materials, products, supplies and services locally, money stays in circulation longer. Tourism related businesses are exactly like other local businesses and benefit the community by implementing revenue retention strategies. Making merchants aware of the local economic benefits of hiring residents and buying materials, products, supplies and services locally is many times enough to keep money circulating in the local economy.

Magnetic Communities value locally produced and grown products from locally-owned and operated businesses. This is why many tourist districts have added farmers' markets and locally made crafts to the mix of available products. This strategy entices both residents and tourists to purchase locally grown produce and crafts. After visiting the farmers market, many shoppers stay downtown to shop and eat, especially if there are other events and attractions to hold their interest.

CHAPTER 8

Resident Strategies

Historically, most residents of a community lived, worked and shopped locally. Today, with modern transportation networks and communication infrastructure, residents have many more options. They may live locally, but use the internet to shop, work from home, run a small business and communicate with friends and family.

When one considers that consumer spending makes up about 70% of GDP (Gross Domestic Product), it is amazing that economic and community developers do not invest more time and effort on this component of the prosperity equation. The primary reason for this lack of attention is that economic and community developers invest their limited time and resources on high profile projects that build support for their programs and funding. Also, they may not appreciate the vital role that residents play in the economic development process. It is important to remember that individuals can choose where to live and how to spend their money. Generally, economic developers do a good job of attracting new businesses and jobs. But, if the workers live and shop in neighboring communities, very little financial benefit accrues to the local economy.

In addition to attracting new money, residents play a key role in keeping money in circulation locally. Even a small up or down shift in the percentage of goods and services purchased locally by residents can substantially impact the amount of money in circulation. To the extent that residents and local leaders are able to influence where individuals live, work and shop, they can impact the community's character, wealth and prosperity.

In some cases, individuals have little or no control over where they spend their money. For example, if a mortgage payment goes to a national lender or an electric bill goes to a regional utility, there is little an individual can do to change things. Also, out of an individual's control are payments that stay in the local economy such as the water bill and the bus fare paid to the city. Where individuals can make a real difference is by purchasing goods and services locally when available, especially from locally owned businesses. Buying fresh produce at the local farmers market and not a national grocery chain: eating at a local restaurant rather than a chain restaurant: purchasing wine from a local vineyard rather than on Amazon, and supporting a local food bank rather than a national or international charity, all keep money in the local economy.

Illustration 19

Residents Commute to Jobs outside the Local Economy

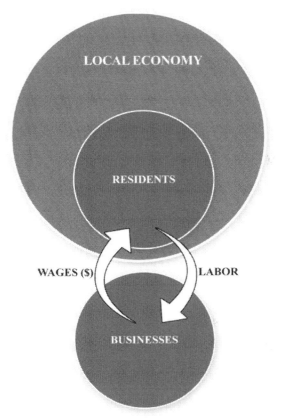

When residents commute to jobs outside the local economy, a substantial portion of their income finds its way back to the local economy. Resident out-commuters, aware that local spending is an effective economic development strategy can help attract money to the local economy by making local purchases when feasible.

Attract Money Strategies

Increase the Number of Out-Commuters

By increasing the number of residents who commute to jobs and earn paychecks outside the community, Magnetic Communities attract new money. Many prosperous suburban communities embrace the idea of being a bedroom community for nearby urban employment centers. Aggressive community development efforts help communities create an excellent quality of life which can be used to recruit and keep out-commuting residents living locally.

Increase the Number of Residents Paid from Outside Sources

Similar to out-commuters, residents paid from outside sources attract new money to the community. While out commuters physically work outside of the community, residents paid from outside sources physically work locally but are paid by companies and organizations located elsewhere. Examples include: Federal workers (military, IRS, VA, etc.), state workers (DOT, health department, school teachers, etc.), college and university employees, telecommuters, and many others. Many of these jobs probably already exist, but are the people filling these jobs living locally? Again, aggressive community development efforts and quality of life enhancements provide the incentives for workers to live locally, rather than in-commute.

Illustration 20

Residents Are Paid from Sources
Outside The Local Economy

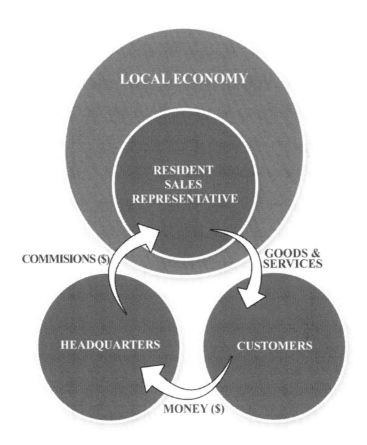

When resident sales representatives, employed by companies headquartered outside the local economy, sell goods and services to outside customers, payments flow through the corporate headquarters, where commissions are calculated and sent to resident sales representatives. If commissions are 50% of goods and services sold and the sale is for $100, the resident sales representative and the local economy are $50 richer.

Question: If customers in Illustration 20 are located inside the local economy, does the impact on the local economy change? Yes! Goods and services are shipped to customers where ever they are located. If customers are located inside the local economy, goods and services still flow to the customers, but payments flow out of the local economy to the corporate headquarters before commissions are calculated and paid to resident sales representatives. Again, let's say commissions are 50% and the sale is for $100. In this scenario, when the customer pays the corporate headquarters, $100 flows out of the local economy and $50 flows back in when commissions are paid. The resident sales representative is still $50 better off but the local economy has lost $50 (-$100 when the local customer pays the corporate headquarters, and +$50 when headquarters pays commissions). Illustration 11, page 81 may help the reader visualize the flow of money.

Many of my business colleagues are employed by businesses located in other communities and states. These sales representatives service a territory, selling goods and services to regional customers. Customer payments are remitted to the company's corporate headquarters, and paychecks are sent to the sales representatives. Almost all of the money earned by the sales representatives is generated from sources outside the local economy and constitutes new money. A few years ago my North Carolina neighbors worked in auditing and collections for companies in New Jersey. They worked locally but were paid from sources outside the local economy. They were paid New Jersey wages which were spent in North Carolina's lower cost of living environment.

Magnetic Communities work to ensure that they have their share of federal and state workers living in their community. Local tax dollars fund these jobs and a proportionate share of the proceeds should be returned to the community in the form of salaries and local spending. In many cases, these individuals are better paid and have more job stability than locals. A list of state and federal agencies with a presence in the community can usually be found in a local directory or online. Compare the list of government operations in your community with those in neighboring towns and counties.

When residents and local businesses pay taxes to state and Federal governments, the expectation is that these tax revenues will be used to benefit taxpayers and communities proportionately. If a community is not receiving its fair share of these tax revenues, it may be time to lobby elected officials to increase the number of government facilities and jobs in the community.

If a community has a military base, reserve unit or National Guard facility, federal and state tax money to support these activities flows into the community. The same holds true for state department of transportation facilities. Another example many economic developers and community leaders fail to recognize are employees of local universities and community colleges funded by state tax dollars and student tuitions. In all of these examples, residents are working locally but collecting paychecks funded from sources outside the community. One final example has both good and bad aspects and includes the chain stores located in almost every community around the country. The list goes on and on: Starbucks, Applebee's, Dollar General, Target, and Walmart; just to name a few. Residents and non-residents work in these branch locations and are paid from the proceeds earned from purchases. Products from outside the local economy are shipped to the branch locations, put on display or on the menu and sold to customers. Hourly wages represent new money to employees and the local economy, while local governments benefit from sales and ad valorem taxes, but that's about it. Few, if any, local products and services end up being stocked, consumed and used in branch stores.

Increase Government Transfer Payments

In today's competitive global economy, poor communities are a reality. Many times, the best strategy for increasing the inflow of money is to insure that residents take full advantage of existing government assistance programs such as Social Security, welfare, unemployment, food stamps, etc. If these residents were working, local economic benefits would probably be greater, but on the positive side, transfer payment recipients are more likely to spend money locally.

Not everyone considers transfer payments contributors to local prosperity, but in some communities these payments represent a substantial source of new money. Even though residents pay taxes and contribute to many of these programs, securing funds from federal and state governments for social programs feel and act a lot like new money.

Illustration 21

Residents Receive and Spend Government
Transfer Payments

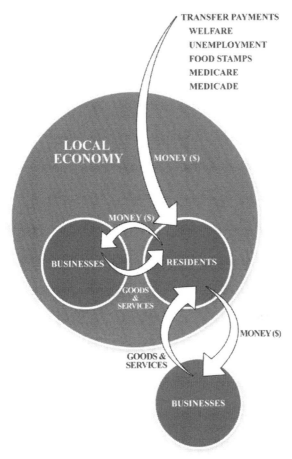

Many economic and community developers pay little attention to government transfer payments received by residents and the local medical establishment. These payments (Welfare, unemployment, food stamps, Medicare, Medicaid, Social Security, etc.) represent new money to the local economy. This new money circulates when residents purchase goods and services from local businesses and exits when residents purchase goods and services from businesses outside the community.

Retain Money Strategies

Make Residents Aware of the Benefits of Spending Locally

Public awareness of Magnetic Community principles is one of the most underrated strategies for retaining money. Businesses and governments are staffed and operated by individuals – hopefully residents – who make hiring, spending and purchasing decisions every day. With an awareness of Magnetic Community principles, private sector employees, business owners, government workers and retirees interested in fostering prosperity can all make informed decisions. An effective awareness campaign promoting the benefits of purchasing local goods and services gives residents a tangible way to get involved in the local economic development process.

When I was a Chamber of Commerce Director, I made every effort to highlight locally owned businesses and local businesses with unique and hard to find products. I was also the chief spokesperson for making sure the public was aware of the economic benefits associated with buying local products and living a Magnetic Community lifestyle.

To illustrate why it is important to get involved with transferees and future residents, I'll use a personal example. When I accepted a job to become the executive director of a county-wide economic development program in eastern N.C., my background and salary were published in the local paper. Over the next six months, I did not receive a single call from a real estate agent, bank, church, social club, furniture store or other retail business. It's in my genes to do the right thing so I started my new life by shopping locally and by immediately establishing a welcome committee as a permanent part of the economic development program. I shudder to think how many opportunities local businesses and organizations missed out on, just because they did not think like a Magnetic Community.

The power of public awareness and word of mouth communication is very effective. For example, I developed an exercise for middle school students where two volunteers, one designated a resident and one designated a non-resident, each were given the same amount of play money and instructed to make several transactions. Halfway through the exercise, the volunteers were asked to count their money. The exercise was structured to ensure that the non-resident student increased his money. The exercise was repeated, allowing the resident student to solicit help from the rest of the class. After much discussion and advice, the fortunes of the volunteers were reversed. I did not know how well the exercise worked until parents started coming up to me with all sorts of questions and stories about why their kids insisted on shopping locally, when in the past they always wanted to go to the mall thirty miles away. Some students even insisted on topping off the gas tank to guarantee they would not have to fill up before returning home.

Spend Locally on Products and Services

Making sure residents understand the wide range of benefits money circulating locally brings with it, motivates them to purchase local goods and services. For example, contracting with a local builder to construct an addition to a resident's home keeps money working locally and adds value to the tax base, which in turn increases the amount of tax revenue local governments have available to provide services.

In reality, communities differ in size and in the variety of goods and services available for sale. A good rule of thumb is to buy what you can locally and fill in the gaps with outside purchases. I always cringe when locals make a road trip to a regional retail center or mall and come back with a car load of items available locally. The same rule of thumb of buying what you can locally holds true for the internet.

Increase the Number and Quality of Products

When goods and services are available locally, residents are less inclined to shop in neighboring towns. Because it is nearly impossible to convince national chain stores to locate a new store if local demographics and traffic counts do not meet minimum requirements. Communities usually have more success convincing existing business owners, local entrepreneurs, retirees or local investors to start new businesses. An additional benefit to this approach is that these new businesses will be locally owned and operated.

Fill Gaps in Product Availability

Many times a community will have a decent selection of retail establishments but finds itself lacking in a few critical areas.

Not having a fine dining restaurant or a home improvement store may require residents to dine and shop in neighboring communities. Again, the real problem arises when these trips turn into daylong events where goods available back home end up in the shopping cart.

If an outflow cannot be eliminated, attempt to reduce its impact on the local economy. Utility payments are a good example. By finding ways to reduce energy consumption, communities also reduce the outflow of money to regional utility providers. Usually for an upfront investment in insulation or conversion to a cheaper fuel, residents are able to reduce their long-term energy costs. Of course, they will have to recoup their upfront investment before any savings are realized. Once break-even is reached, residents and businesses will continue to pay less for energy, increasing the amount of money they have to spend and reducing the amount of money flowing out of the local economy. Finding a local, state or national energy subsidy program decreases the upfront cost to consumers and shortens the time it takes to break-even.

Illustration 22

**Residents Purchase Goods and Services from
Local Businesses**

When residents purchase goods and services from local businesses, money circulates in the local economy and is retained. If the recipients of this spending also make purchases locally, money remains in circulation, providing additional economic benefits.

Illustration 23

Residents Purchase Goods and Services from Businesses Outside the Local Economy

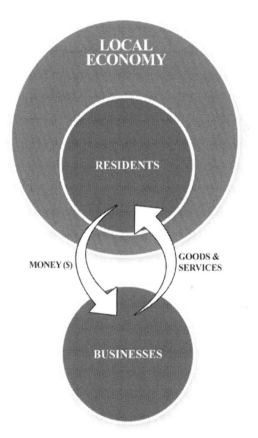

When residents purchase goods and services from businesses located outside the local economy or online, money exits the community and is no longer available for spending. Not only is the initial spending a drain on the local economy, but also the potential spending from money not retained locally.

Residents play an important role in both the attraction and retention of money. Making residents aware of their role is a fundamental strategy for Magnetic Communities.

CHAPTER 9

Retiree Strategies

Almost all communities have retirees, but not all communities recognize the economic benefits and potential resources they bring to the local economy. Many retirees bring a lifetime of savings and a steady stream of retirement income to this new phase of their lives. Similar to working residents, retirees spend money on groceries, eating out, entertainment, housing, transportation, home repairs, etc. In fact, many retirees continue to work. In addition to a steady flow of income and withdrawals from savings, retirees also purchase homes, recreation vehicles, boats and new cars, all of which stimulate the local economy.

Workers getting ready to retire may decide to stay where they are or move to be near friends, family and neighbors. They may also decide to move to an area with a warmer climate and a lower cost of living. The decisions they make impact the communities where they live. Even though retirees may not be working, in most cases they receive monthly income from a variety of sources. Depending on their situation, retirees attract new money from Social Security, pensions, savings, consulting work, business ownership, investments, etc. Their purchasing habits may change, but they continue to receive and spend money. It is important to remember that residents who move and retire outside the community take their income streams and savings with them.

Medicare payments to local doctors and hospitals also represent new money for the local economy. Even though Medicare is funded by governments, employees, businesses, and beneficiaries, the money is held by the Federal Government until retirees need it for medical expenses. If residents move when they retire, Medicare payments become new money for the retiree's new community.

Magnetic Communities focus retiree strategies on creating senior friendly environments with a high quality of life. Whether staying where they are or moving, retirees are looking for great places to live with a wide variety of amenities and attributes. Some of these include:

- Mild climate
- Scenic beauty
- Low cost of living
- Recreation, shopping and dining opportunities
- Medical services
- A range of housing options at reasonable prices
- Cultural, social and spiritual opportunities
- Continuing education
- Safe, quiet neighborhoods
- Transportation options

Appropriate housing is a high priority for many seniors. When people get older, their housing needs change. For example, as children move out of the house to attend college, work or start a family, aging couples, now empty nesters, may want to continue living in the area but not in a large home with multiple sets of stairs and a yard. They may look for a smaller, single level home in a nearby development. Later on they may want to downsize even further to a one-story condominium without maintenance responsibilities. Next, they may look for an assisted living facility and then for a nursing home. Most retirees want to stay in their homes and communities as long as possible but may be forced to move if they cannot find appropriate housing. By insuring a continuum of housing options, the likelihood retirees and their income streams remain in the community increase. Many home builders and developers do not recognize the need to provide a continuum of housing, but when presented with the opportunity to sell homes and rent apartments, they may be convinced to give it a try.

Whether new to the community or longtime residents, retirees have skills, expertise, career experience, professional connections and social networks. These skills and contacts represent potential resources for communities. Retirees also provide local expertise and knowledge that otherwise would have to be purchased outside the community. Magnetic communities actively work to identify volunteer opportunities for retirees and to encourage civic organizations, churches, nonprofits, chambers of commerce, etc., to welcome retirees and to help them get involved. Magnetic Communities understand and appreciate the potential economic benefits and resources retirees bring to the local economy.

Many retirees dream of starting and owning their own business. Retirees looking for "encore" careers can be tremendous assets; but because developing entrepreneurship programs are time consuming and do not produce a big groundbreaking ceremony; many communities fail to allocate resources for entrepreneurship and small business development. Assisting local retirees start businesses is an important Magnetic Community strategy.

Overall, retirees are living longer, working longer and earning paychecks longer. In anticipation of retirement, many business owners seek to move their businesses and/or their residences to new locations. If communities add both retirees and businesses at the same time, the economic benefits extend for years into the future. Even if retirees do not move their businesses, they may retain a financial interest, creating streams of income for their new communities.

Many economic and community developers consider retirees permanent tourists. This may be a valid comparison, but one rural county manager told me that tourists are fine because they come, spend money and leave; retirees on the other hand are a completely different story; they come and stay, expecting the same levels of service as their previous high tax locations. In large numbers, retirees also have a tendency to alter the local culture. Two final notes: as retirees age, they tend to require more social services, which comes at a cost to local governments, and, in large numbers, relocating retirees can create financial disparities between themselves and longtime residents.

Attract Money Strategies

Increase the Number of Retirees

The obvious revenue attraction strategy is to increase the number of local retirees who have money to spend. As mentioned earlier, retirees bring pensions, savings, Social Security, Medicare, Medicaid, business income, etc. to a community. If a community recruits new retirees from outside the community, or retains resident-retirees, much of their local spending will come from new money attracted to the local economy. The real economic threat from retiring residents is that they move away and take their income and spending with them.

Recruit Younger, Amenity-Seeking Retirees

Retirees who move from one location to another in retirement are usually: younger, healthier, and wealthier. They are generally looking for a specific set of amenities and lifestyle attributes to fill their retirement goals. When marketing communities to potential retirees, it is important to not overlook the obvious. Local leaders and residents accustomed to mild climates, scenic beauty and an array of outdoor recreational opportunities may not see these as retirement assets, but rather something available in all communities. Other retirees may want to live in urban areas with cultural amenities, public transportation and fine dining.

Develop a Senior-Friendly Environment

Communities that plan and design neighborhoods with seniors in mind usually create environments welcoming to all residents. Some states have developed retirement community designation and certification programs to help communities develop senior friendly environments and to help potential retirees identify the best possible retirement locations for their needs.

Illustration 24

Retirees Receive Retirement Income

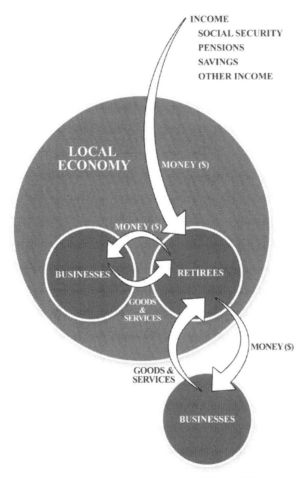

When retirees receive retirement income (Social Security, savings, pensions, etc.) they are free to spend the money on goods and services inside or outside the local economy. Money spent in the local economy stays in circulation locally, while money spent outside the local economy is lost to future spending and economic benefits. Because a substantial amount of retiree income, such as Social Security, Medicare and pensions is received from outside the local economy, it feels and acts a lot like new money. Local

retirees are residents of the community and their income/spending produces similar results.

Retain Money Strategies

Increase the Amount of Money Retirees Spend Locally

By making sure that merchants stock and provide the goods and services seniors want to purchase, Magnetic Communities ensure that retiree spending stays in the local economy. Development organizations can encourage local spending by highlighting local companies, their products and services. Many communities use traditional economic development strategies to recruit, expand, retain and start businesses that provide the products, services and amenities sought by retirees.

Magnetic Communities identify and promote investment opportunities for local retirees. Retirees who have money invested on Wall Street may want to diversify their portfolio and invest on Main Street. Magnetic Communities encourage and facilitate interactions between potential retiree-investors and investment opportunities.

The most common downfall of retiree-based economic development strategies is to not provide the local services and products retirees want to purchase. As a result, a positive stream of retirement income enters the community and is immediately countered by a negative stream of money leaving the community when retirees shop in neighboring communities. Also, as retirees age, they tend to drive less and look for goods and services closer to home. If unavailable, they may choose to move.

Ensure that Older Residents Retire Locally

Similar to business retention, it is usually easier to retain local retirees than to recruit new ones. Not all retirees are looking for the same things in retirement. If a community has many of the attributes retirees are looking for in a retirement community and retiree attraction is part of the community's economic development strategy, trying to keep retirees in the community is a good way to advance prosperity goals. If residents approaching retirement age pack up and move to the beach when they are in their late 50's or early 60's, communities may lose the benefits of 20 to 30 years of retirement income and spending.

CHAPTER 10

Government Strategies

Most residents and community leaders understand that taxes are necessary to fund local, state and federal governments, but how many of them think of taxes and government services in terms of money flow? When locally owned businesses and residents pay taxes and fees to their local governments, money circulates in the community, but no new money is attracted. The best communities can do to leverage the economic benefits of local tax dollars is to keep the money circulating locally for as long as possible. Taxes paid to state and federal governments represent outflows of money. Magnetic Communities work to insure that local businesses and residents receive their fair share of these taxes back in the form of services and infrastructure.

When combined: local tax revenues, charges and fees usually represent the largest source of income for local governments. Knowing that most of a town's revenue is generated locally and does not represent new money should make keeping it in the local economy a top priority. To insure that local tax dollars used to pay employees remain in the community, local governments should require that local government employees and top managers live in the local jurisdiction. Do not be fooled into thinking that local government paychecks to resident-employees represent new money.

Local governments do attract a limited amount of new money from grants, intergovernmental transfers and local taxes paid by outside businesses with investments and operations in the jurisdiction. New money is also generated from nonresidents with second homes and investments in the jurisdiction. It is important that Magnetic Communities determine where local governments are getting their money and where it is being spent. Counting on a resident to win the lottery is probably not the best strategy for attracting new money.

Local governments are subject to Freedom of Information laws that require information be made available to the public upon request. Public information laws allow individuals and businesses access to the information necessary to determine where tax dollars are being generated and where they are being spent. For example, a quick look at accounts payable will identify payments to companies located both inside and outside the local jurisdiction. In many communities, local governments are one of the largest employers, making their budget an integral part of the local economy.

Illustration 25

Local Governments Collect Taxes from Residents and Local Businesses

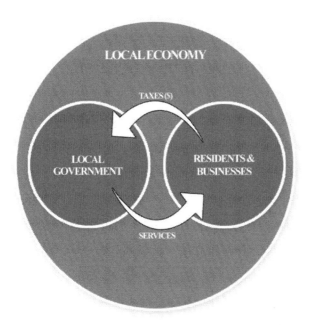

Because local governments are part of the local economy and because they generate income primarily by collecting taxes from local businesses and residents, there is little opportunity to attract new money. The best communities can do to leverage the benefits of local tax revenue is to spend it locally and keep it in circulation.

Illustration 26

Federal and State Governments Collect Taxes from Residents and Local Businesses

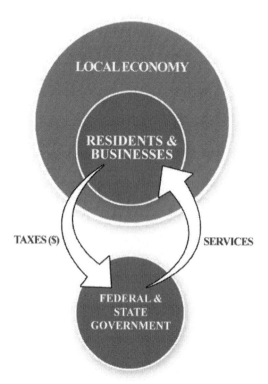

In contrast to local governments, when federal and state governments collect taxes from residents and local businesses, money flows out of the local economy. If the community receives its fair share of federal and state taxes in return for things like roads, national security, parks, etc., the process is working as intended. Overages positively impact the local economy, while shortages are a drain.

Attract Money Strategies

Maximize Inflow of Money

Many local governments collect fees from outside the local jurisdiction for utilities, recreation, etc. They may also collect non tax revenues from fines and court costs, etc. Many public and private agencies, along with nonprofits, provide competitive grants to help achieve their mission. For example, state agencies may offer grants to help develop local parks and playgrounds, while the Federal Government may offer transportation planning grants. In addition, a local jurisdiction may get paid by a neighboring jurisdiction to house prisoners or to provide water services. In these cases, local governments act like private businesses and provide services for a fee to customers outside the local jurisdiction, creating an inflow of money.

A variety of grants are available from state and Federal sources (www.grants.gov). Local residents and businesses fund these grant programs when they pay taxes. It is the responsibility of local governments to make sure they receive their fair share in return. This may entail lobbying elected officials, and hiring or contracting with a grant writer. In fact, communities with effective grant writing programs can not only get their fair share of taxes back, but many times get more than their fair share. Just think about it, for every community that comes up short, others are making money.

Once a grant is awarded, implementation and administration can be a challenge, especially for small communities. If an outside consultant is hired, money will flow out of the community. But without a qualified grant writer and administrator, a community may not receive the grant in the first place or may run into compliance issues, which can be costly to correct. Even though local grant writing, implementation and administration are ideal, increasing a community's chances of being awarded a grant and staying out of trouble administrating the grant may be worth the cost of an outside consultant.

Maximize Benefits from the Transfer of Intergovernmental Funds

Local governments must make sure they are receiving and making the most of intergovernmental transfers. These transfers from one level of government to another are most often used to fund general government or specific programs. For example, in North Carolina, pay for public school teachers is funded by local, state and federal governments. If a community has 200 school teachers on the payroll and only 100 of them live locally, the community is only getting half of its tax money back. Magnetic Communities consider this situation an opportunity to develop and implement strategies that attract school teachers to live in the local jurisdiction. If 50 school teachers living outside the community can be convinced to relocate, the equivalent of 50 new jobs is added to the local economy.

Retain Money Strategies

Identify Locally Available Materials, Supplies and Services

When available, local governments should make every effort to purchase goods, services and raw materials locally. Also, make it a priority to consider local vendors when awarding contracts. For instance, many local governments provide residents with garbage collection. Over time, as costs rise, local jurisdictions are tempted to contract with regional and national companies to take over these services. Local taxes or fees still pay for the service, but rather than paying local workers, local governments pay outside companies and their workers, creating an outflow of money. Assisting local citizens start a garbage collection business or organizing several small businesses to bid on the local contract keeps money in the local economy.

Governments and politicians love to talk about saving money, but if the savings are achieved by contracting with low bidders from outside the local jurisdiction, the savings are probably on paper only.

Local governments that try to save money by paying as little as possible for materials, supplies and services, regardless of where they are purchased, are probably not retaining as much money as possible. To illustrate, let's say the town council votes to outsource a maintenance function to the low bidder, a company in a neighboring town. Let's also say that by awarding a $200,000 contract, the town eliminates a $250,000 budget item, saving the town $50,000. The first thing to recognize is that the $250,000 budget line item represented three local jobs and spending on locally purchased services and supplies. The town may save $50,000 and reduce the budget, but it lost $200,000 in local wages, spending, sales taxes, and multipliers created by the spending. A more carefully worded request for proposals, one that gives local firms a priority, may result in a local firm winning the contract. In this case, the town still saves money but payments to the contractor stay in the local economy. Purchasing materials, products and services at the lowest price possible does not always save communities money.

Hire Residents and Require Transferees to Live within the Local Jurisdiction

Living in the local jurisdiction should be a requirement for local government employees. The next time you're driving around, notice the number of emergency and law enforcement vehicles parked in driveways outside the jurisdiction stenciled on the door.

When local governments hire employees without regard to where they live, local tax dollars are inevitably going to flow out of the community. By establishing a policy, formal or informal, that local government positions must be filled: first by qualified residents, second by qualified applicants willing to relocate, and third by non-residents, maximizes the probability that local tax dollars used to pay employees remain in the local economy.

Illustration 27

Local Governments Purchase Goods and Services

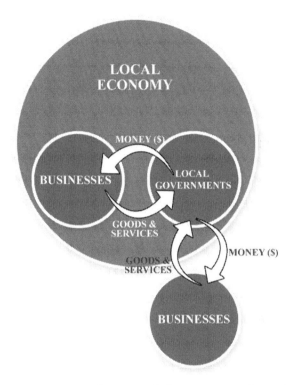

Local governments need many of the same goods and services required by private sector businesses, and like other businesses they can price and make purchases inside or outside the local economy. If purchased locally, money is retained and circulates, if not purchased locally, money flows out of the community and is no longer available to produce economic benefits.

Illustration 28

Local Governments Employ Residents and Nonresidents

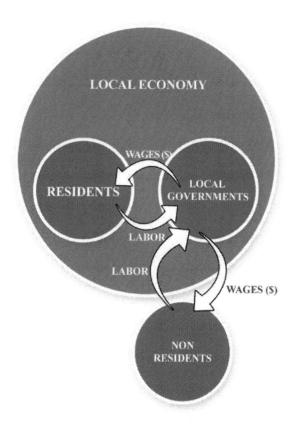

Illustration 28 shows the flow of money when local governments employ and pay wages to residents and to nonresidents. Money paid to residents continues to circulate, while money paid to non-residents flows out of the local economy and is lost to future spending.

A Fish Story

Part One

A fish swimming in the ocean has little or no economic value until it is caught. Once in the boat, the fisherman has something he can sell to the local fish market. The fish market adds value by cleaning the fish and preparing it for the local restaurant. The restaurant continues to add value by cooking the fish and serving it to a customer. To further set the stage for Illustrations 29, 30 and 31, let's say the fisherman gets $5 from the fish market for the fish, the fish market gets $10 from the restaurant, and the restaurant gets $20 from the customer for a fish dinner. In all three illustrations, a fisherman, fish market and restaurant add value and make money, but depending on whether a resident or a nonresident enjoys the fish dinner, the outcome for the local economy is quite different. Consider the following illustrations.

Illustration 29

A Fish Story – Community Retains Money

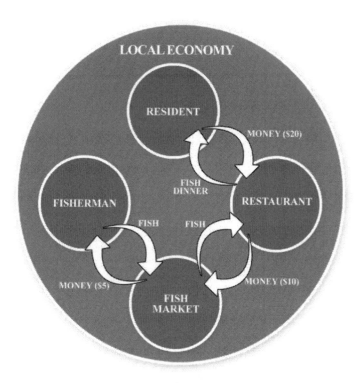

When locally caught and processed fish are sold to local restaurants and served to residents, money circulates in the community but no new money is attracted to the local economy. This does not mean that local businesses have not benefited economically. The restaurant sold a fish dinner to a resident for $20.00, the fish market sold a processed fish to the restaurant for $10.00 and the fisherman sold a freshly caught fish to the fish market for $5.00.

Illustration 30

A Fish Story – Community Attracts Money

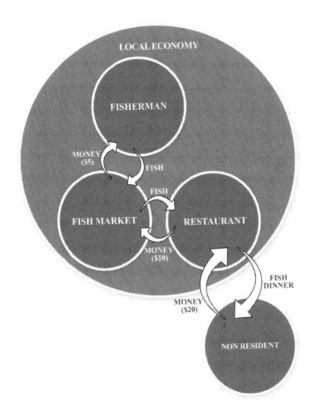

When locally caught and processed fish are sold to local restaurants and served to nonresidents, new money is attracted to the local economy and the community has more money to spend. In Illustration 30, the restaurant, fish market and fisherman all make money, but this time the community also attracts $20.00.

Part Two

A day later, the local fisherman gets a tip that the fish are biting twenty miles up the coast. He makes the trip and catches another fish he can sell for $5.00. But, because he is further up the coast, the closest fish market and restaurant are not in his home port. The fisherman is in a hurry so he sells the fish and receives $5.00 from an out of town fish market; the fish market in turn receives $10.00 from an out of town restaurant and later that evening the restaurant serves a $20.00 fish dinner to a resident from the fisherman's home port.

In this case, because the local fisherman receives $5.00 from an out of town fish market, both he and the fishing village are $5.00 better off. This is assuming the fisherman spends the $5.00 back in his home port. Because the fish market and the restaurant are both outside the local economy, the restaurant's purchase of the fish from the fish market does not add to or subtract from the local flow of money. If a resident on his way home to the fishing village orders, eats and pays for the fish dinner at the out of town restaurant, $20.00 flows out of the community and the local economy has a net $15.00 less to spend.

Illustration 31

A Fish Story – Community Loses Money

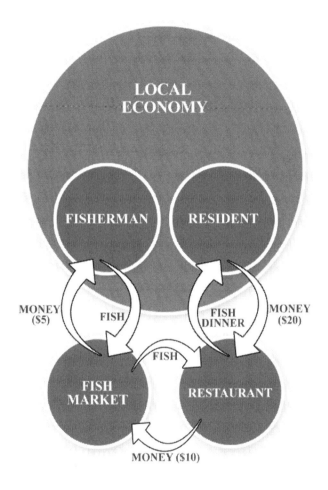

When locally caught fish are processed outside the local economy, sold to outside restaurants and served to residents, the community loses money, primarily because two value added processes (cleaning and cooking) are completed by businesses outside the local economy.

This basic scenario plays out every day in communities where fishermen and fish are plentiful; but seafood restaurants are nowhere to be found. It also occurs when communities with places to eat lack a seafood restaurant, forcing residents to leave the community to enjoy a fish dinner. Filling gaps in the local availability of goods and services is a Magnetic Community strategy for retaining money in the local economy.

For example, if the fishing community in Illustration 31 can establish a fish market and/or a restaurant in the local economy, additional value will be added to the fish, improving the money flow equation for the fishing community. Finally, if the owners of the restaurant are able to attract outside visitors and tourists to the restaurant, both the restaurant and the local economy will have more money to spend.

Summary

Magnetic Communities take a different approach to economic and community development. Rather than working to attract businesses and create jobs, Magnetic Communities work to create a superior quality of life and to provide current and future residents with the resources necessary to succeed. Communities looking to prosper locally in a global economy implement economic development strategies that create a positive cash flow by attracting and retaining money.

As stated in the Preface, and worth repeating, Magnetic Communities include towns, cities, counties, states and regions that excel in attracting and retaining money, a process that creates a positive cash flow. Because local businesses, residents and local governments have an ever increasing amount of money to spend, they prosper. Prosperity allows businesses to grow, create jobs and pay dividends; it allows residents to improve their personal well-being by providing the money necessary for better housing, healthcare, education, leisure activities, etc.; and it allows governments to generate the tax revenue necessary to provide the services residents and businesses need to succeed.

By embracing the Magnetic Community approach to economic development, communities are able to identify and evaluate strategies that create prosperity. The term "Magnetic Communities" serves as a reminder to residents, local leaders and economic developers that money must be both attracted and retained to create prosperity. Hopefully, over time, the term "Magnetic Communities" will be used as a catchphrase for local development strategies that attract and retain money.

Community prosperity is comprised of community wealth and personal well-being. Communities cannot create prosperity. Individuals must prosper for communities to prosper, and communities must prosper for governments to prosper.

The economic development goal of Magnetic Communities is to advance prosperity and to improve local quality of life. The overall objective is to create a positive cash flow, or a net gain of money flowing into the local economy. This is accomplished by (1) increasing the amount of money flowing into the community, by (2) increasing the amount of money circulating locally and by (3) decreasing the amount of money flowing out of the community. Local economic development success is measured by the number of newly employed residents, the value of newly awarded local contracts and the increase in local spending, not in the total number of new jobs and capital investment.

Simplifying the economic development process empowers both local leaders and residents to get involved. The reason many economic development strategies and programs languish is because they are too complicated and not fully understood by residents, businesses and governments. Small actions by many people make a big difference in creating prosperous communities. It takes a community working together to unleash the power of community.

More involvement by residents does not mean more work, but rather a greater awareness of what creates prosperity and what actions residents can take to move the community closer to its goal. One of the reasons residents are left out of the economic development process is because they are lumped together into groups such as business leaders, educators, school administrators, blue collar workers, elected officials, retirees, etc., which takes away from their individuality as members of the community. Each of these groups is made up of individuals. These individuals, hopefully residents of the community, have multiple roles to play. For example, a local plant manager has a role as both a business leader and as a resident.

Throughout *Magnetic Communities*, reference is made to five groups, which include: businesses, tourists, residents, retirees and local governments. Individual members of these groups have decision making power to attract and retain money. These groups are made up of individuals who have influence over how the group operates and where they spend and invest. For example, let's not forget that individuals make purchasing decisions, not companies.

In the beginning of *Magnetic Communities*, I stated that my personal long-term economic development quest was to determine why some communities thrive and prosper and others struggle and decline. My conclusion, after a 25-year career in economic development, is that by implementing economic development strategies that attract and retain money, communities are able to create a positive cash flow and prosper. Communities that focus development strategies on attracting businesses and jobs: without regard to the flow of money, struggle and decline.

When a new business opens, residents think of increased sales, economic growth, new investment and more jobs. But in reality, this is not always the case. To illustrate how two similar projects can produce very different results, consider Illustrations 32 and 33.

Illustration 32

Best Case Business Scenario

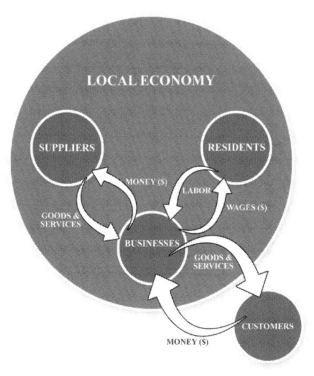

In the best case scenario, a local entrepreneur or group of local investors start a business, contract with local suppliers, hire residents and sell products and services to customers outside the local economy, which maximizes the amount of money attracted and retained. When local businesses sell products and services to outside customers, they attract new money, which is used to pay local suppliers and resident labor. This ends up being a best case scenario because money is attracted and retained in the local economy. Money does not flow out of the community.

Illustration 33

Worst Case Business Scenario

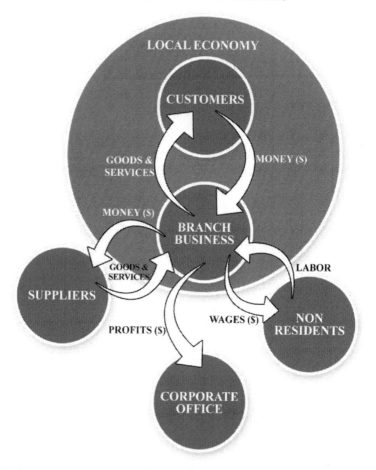

In the worst case scenario, an outside entrepreneur or group of outside investors start a local business, sell products to local businesses, remit profits to the corporate office, contract with outside suppliers and hire non-resident workers.

This worst case scenario plays out more often than people think. For example, when a new industrial project locates in the local industrial park, economic developers are hoping that suppliers will also locate in the park or at least nearby. When this happens, the community, local governments, businesses and residents all feel like they've hit the jackpot. But, by following the money trail and flow of money, the economic benefits and its impact on prosperity may be minimal. First of all, if the new supplier receives the same incentives as the industrial prospect, local governments are probably not going to fully benefit from tax revenues for quite some time. Second, if the supplier is providing products and services exclusively to the new manufacturer, the community is not attracting any new money. Third, if the new supplier gets its raw materials, supplies and labor from outside the local economy, money exits the community. Finally, money flows out of the community when profits are remitted to the corporate headquarters.

The preceding two scenarios are simplifications of what happens in real life. But again, understanding the basics of money flow allows members of the community to identify, evaluate and follow money trails for individual projects.

So what can individuals do to help create Magnetic Communities?

As a Working Resident or Resident-Retiree:

- Purchase local products and services - spend locally.

- Patronize locally owned and operated businesses.

- Tell friends and neighbors about local companies with excellent products, services and hard to find items.

- When warranted, write positive online reviews for local stores, contractors, services, etc.

- Increase local awareness of Magnetic Community principles and strategies that attract and retain money – start a conversation.

- Invest locally rather than on Wall Street.

- Start a small business.

- Invite non-resident coworkers and friends to attend local events that promote the community.

- Retire locally, encourage others to retire locally.

- Get involved, become a leader.

As a Local Business Owner, Manager and Employee:

- Sell more goods and services outside the local economy and to tourists.

- Purchase materials, supplies and services locally, especially from locally owned and operated businesses.

- Hire qualified residents and request that new hires relocate to the community.

- Seek out and sell more locally grown and produced products.

As a Local Government Manager, Employee and Elected Official:

- Purchase materials, supplies and services locally, especially from locally owned and operated businesses.

- Hire qualified residents and request that new hires relocate to the local jurisdiction.

- Apply for grants.

- Maximize outside revenue.

Get started today! No permission required.

~Build a Magnetic Community~

About the Author

Larry Moolenaar is a life-long economic developer with more than 25 years of experience in business recruitment, strategic planning, community development, project management and consulting.

Mr. Moolenaar worked as a Senior Project manager for Atlanta-based Georgia Power Company's Economic and Community Development Department where he: directed and managed corporate relocation projects, implemented the national marketing plan, prepared comparative location and site selection studies, and executed the company's small business development program.

As a Business Consultant for the University of South Carolina's Small Business Development Center, Larry provided managerial and technical assistance to small businesses, developed business plans and secured financing for both existing and pre-venture companies in the Charleston, SC area.

In Newberry, SC, Larry directed the activities of the Newberry Chamber of Commerce, the Newberry Development Board, Visitor's Center and the Downtown Development Association. He assisted community leaders develop and implement an economic and community development strategy, which resulted in a new industrial park that attracted five international companies in five years. Larry was recognized by the South Carolina House of Representatives for his economic development leadership in Newberry County, resulting in $190 million in new investments, 1,500 jobs, $1 million in infrastructure grants, $10.2 million in voter-approved capital projects and a 72-room hotel on the square in downtown Newberry.

Larry's next stop was Lenoir County, NC where he served as the County's economic developer and was responsible for industrial recruitment, plant expansion, business retention and small business development. While in Lenoir County, Larry completed an industrial site feasibility study and initiated a county-wide strategic planning process. He also developed incentive policies for relocating and expanding companies.

As Executive Director of the Eastern Carolina Council of Governments in New Bern, NC, Mr. Moolenaar managed a nine-county regional development organization that provided human, planning and economic development services to 62 local governments and more than 600,000 residents. The Council's services included strategic planning, grant writing, grant administration, community planning, senior services, transportation planning and a variety of other consulting services. During this period, Larry's interaction with local elected officials and economic developers generated the idea for Magnetic Communities.

Mr. Moolenaar earned a Bachelor of Business Administration degree from West Georgia University in Carrollton, GA and a Master of Business Administration degree from Georgia State University in Atlanta, GA. Larry is a graduate of the Economic Development Institute in Norman, OK.

52399522R00102

Made in the USA
Columbia, SC
08 March 2019